First World War
and Army of Occupation
War Diary
France, Belgium and Germany

29 DIVISION
Headquarters, Branches and Services
General Staff
1 March 1916 - 31 March 1916

WO95/2280/1

The Naval & Military Press Ltd
www.nmarchive.com
Published in association with The National Archives

Published by

The Naval & Military Press Ltd

Unit 10 Ridgewood Industrial Park,

Uckfield, East Sussex,

TN22 5QE England

Tel: +44 (0) 1825 749494

www.naval-military-press.com

www.nmarchive.com

This diary has been reprinted in facsimile from the original. Any imperfections are inevitably reproduced and the quality may fall short of modern type and cartographic standards.

© **Crown Copyright**
Images reproduced by permission of The National Archives, London, England, 2015.

Contents

Document type	Place/Title	Date From	Date To
Heading	29th Division General Staff Mar-Aug 1916		
Heading	Arrived Marseilles From Egypt 20th March 1916. General Staff 29th Division March 1916		
Heading	War Diary General Staff 29th Division For The month of March 1916. Volume XIII		
War Diary		01/03/1916	31/03/1916
Heading	Appendices For February 1916		
Miscellaneous	A Form. Messages And Signals.		
Miscellaneous	(1 Copy To 29th Division).	03/02/1916	03/02/1916
Miscellaneous	Officer i/c., 29th Divisional Cyclist Company Appx 1	04/02/1916	04/02/1916
Miscellaneous	A.D.M.S.	07/02/1916	07/02/1916
Miscellaneous	29th Divisional Cyclist Company.	04/02/1916	04/02/1916
Miscellaneous	86th.87th And 88th Brigades.	04/02/1916	04/02/1916
Miscellaneous	C.R.A. C.R.E.	04/02/1916	04/02/1916
Miscellaneous	86th Bde	04/02/1916	04/02/1916
Miscellaneous	Staff Captain 87th Infty Bde	05/02/1916	05/02/1916
Miscellaneous	29th Division.	05/02/1916	05/02/1916
Miscellaneous	O.C. 29th Div Sig. Co. R.E.	11/02/1916	11/02/1916
Miscellaneous	Time Table. for Officers on Course of Instructions		
Miscellaneous	C.R.E. 29th Division.	04/02/1916	04/02/1916
Miscellaneous		05/02/1915	05/02/1915
Miscellaneous	29th Division	05/02/1916	05/02/1916
Miscellaneous	Proposed Programme of Training for Specialists	05/02/1916	05/02/1916
Miscellaneous	Staff Capt 87th Inf. Bde.	05/02/1916	05/02/1916
Miscellaneous	Staff Captain 87th Infy Brigade	02/02/1916	02/02/1916
Miscellaneous	29th Division	08/02/1916	08/02/1916
Miscellaneous	29th Div.	22/02/1916	22/02/1916
Miscellaneous	General Officer Commanding. Alexandria District.	26/02/1916	26/02/1916
Operation(al) Order(s)	29th Divisional Order No. 21	27/02/1916	27/02/1916
Miscellaneous	Instruction RE Embarkation 29th Division	26/02/1916	26/02/1916
Miscellaneous	A Form. Messages And Signals.	27/02/1916	27/02/1916
Miscellaneous	C Form (Quadruplicate). Messages And Signals.	28/11/1916	28/11/1916
Miscellaneous	A Form. Messages And Signals.	29/02/1916	29/02/1916
Miscellaneous	A Form. Messages And Signals.		
Miscellaneous	General Headquarters. Mediterranean Expeditionary. Force.	26/02/1916	26/02/1916
Miscellaneous	Headquarters, 9th Corps.	29/02/1916	29/02/1916
Miscellaneous	A Form. Messages And Signals.	26/02/1916	26/02/1916
Operation(al) Order(s)	10th (Indian) Division Operation Order No. 17.	29/02/1916	29/02/1916
Miscellaneous			
Miscellaneous	Headquarters, 9th Corps, Suez.	29/02/1916	29/02/1916
Miscellaneous	Appx I 1-12		
Miscellaneous	Appendix I	01/03/1916	01/03/1916
Miscellaneous	The General Officer Commanding 9th. Army Corps, Suez.	01/03/1916	01/03/1916
Miscellaneous	A Form. Messages And Signals.		
Miscellaneous	C Form (Quadruplicate). Messages And Signals.		
Miscellaneous	A Form. Messages And Signals.		
Miscellaneous	C Form (Quadruplicate). Messages And Signals.		
Miscellaneous	B Form. Messages And Signals.	13/11/1916	13/11/1916

Miscellaneous	A Form. Messages And Signals.		
Miscellaneous	C Form (Quadruplicate). Messages And Signals.	12/11/1916	12/11/1916
Miscellaneous	B Form. Messages And Signals.	13/11/1916	13/11/1916
Miscellaneous	A Form. Messages And Signals.		
Miscellaneous	Headquarters, 9th Army Corps.	29/02/1916	29/02/1916
Miscellaneous	Staff Officer Q.M.G. Branch		
Miscellaneous	A.A. & Q.M.G., 29th Division.	01/03/1916	01/03/1916
Miscellaneous	C Form (Triplicate). Messages And Signals.		
Miscellaneous	A Form. Messages And Signals.		
Miscellaneous	For Officers Use Only.		
Miscellaneous	Appx 2 1-2		
Miscellaneous	Headquarters, 9th Corps. Appendix 2	01/03/1916	01/03/1916
Miscellaneous			
Miscellaneous	To. G.O.C. 9th Corps (Cipher). No. 4405.	01/03/1915	01/03/1915
Miscellaneous	Appx. 3 1-5		
Operation(al) Order(s)	Force Order No. 12 by General Sir Archibald Murray K.C.B., K.C.M.G., C.V.O., D.S.O. Commander-in-Chief, Mediterranean Expeditionary Force. Appendix 3	03/03/1916	03/03/1916
Miscellaneous	A Form. Messages And Signals.		
Miscellaneous	B Form. Messages And Signals.	13/11/1916	13/11/1916
Miscellaneous	A Form. Messages And Signals.		
Miscellaneous	The General Officer Commanding 9th. Corps, Suez.	03/03/1916	03/03/1916
Miscellaneous	Details 29th Division & 31st Division to embark at Port Said,	03/03/1916	03/03/1916
Miscellaneous			
Miscellaneous	List of Officers Proceeding on Night 4/5 to Port said for Embarkation		
Miscellaneous	A Form. Messages And Signals.		
Miscellaneous	Messages And Signals.		
Miscellaneous	29th Division.	03/03/1916	03/03/1916
Miscellaneous	Appx. 4 1-3		
Miscellaneous	O.S. 352		
Miscellaneous	A.D.O.S. 9th Corps. Appendix 4.	04/03/1916	04/03/1916
Miscellaneous	B Form. Messages And Signals.		
Miscellaneous	Appx. 5 1-3		
Miscellaneous	G.O.C. 9th Corps. Suez Appendix 5	06/03/1916	06/03/1916
Miscellaneous	G.O.C. 9th Corps. Suez.	06/03/1916	06/03/1916
Miscellaneous	Unit: 29th Division	06/03/1916	06/03/1916
Miscellaneous			
Miscellaneous	The following officers and other ranks embarked on "H.M.T. Manitou" at Port Said on 5th March 1916		
Miscellaneous	Appx 6 1-4		
Miscellaneous	The General Officer Commanding 9th. Army Corps. Appendix 6.	06/03/1916	06/03/1916
Miscellaneous	29th. Division. 1st.Flight, to embark Alexandria March 8th		
Miscellaneous	General Officer Commanding, 9th Army Corps.	06/03/1916	06/03/1916
Miscellaneous	General Officer Commanding, 9th Corps, Suez.	07/03/1916	07/03/1916
Miscellaneous	H.Q. 29th Division.	07/03/1916	07/03/1916
Miscellaneous	1st.Flight, 29th, Division From Suez To Alexandria		
Miscellaneous	Train Timings for The Move of 1st Flight 29th Division on March 8/9th		
Operation(al) Order(s)	Operation Order No. 22 by Major General H. de B. de Lisle C.B. D.S.O. Commanding 29th Division	07/03/1916	07/03/1916
Miscellaneous	Allotment Of Berthing Accomodation		
Miscellaneous	9th Army Corps.	07/03/1916	07/03/1916

Miscellaneous	29th Division. 1st Flight to embark Alexandria,	09/03/1916	09/03/1916
Miscellaneous	C Form (Original). Messages And Signals.		
Miscellaneous	A.Q.M.G. IXth Corps.	07/03/1916	07/03/1916
Miscellaneous	Appx. 7		
Miscellaneous	A Form. Messages And Signals.		
Miscellaneous	C Form (Duplicate). Messages And Signals.	08/11/1916	08/11/1916
Miscellaneous	C Form (Duplicate). Messages And Signals.		
Miscellaneous	A Form. Messages And Signals.		
Miscellaneous	Headquarters, 87th Brigade.	08/03/1916	08/03/1916
Miscellaneous	The Units to be embarked are.		
Miscellaneous	29th Division. 1st Flight to embark Alexandria,	09/03/1916	09/03/1916
Miscellaneous	Herewith Train Timings referred to in Para. 1 Operation Order No. 22	08/03/1916	08/03/1916
Miscellaneous	Move of 1st Flight, 29th Division From Suez to Alexandria		
Miscellaneous	Train Timings for The Move of 1st Flight 29th Division on March 8/9th		
Miscellaneous	Appx 8 1-5		
Miscellaneous	Appendix 8		
Miscellaneous	The General Officer Commanding 9th. Army Corps.	08/03/1916	08/03/1916
Miscellaneous	Allotment Of Berthing Accomodation		
Miscellaneous	The General Officer Commanding 9th Corps.	08/03/1916	08/03/1916
Miscellaneous	Move of 1st. Flight, 29th. Division		
Miscellaneous	Summary Of Cipher Message.	09/06/1916	09/06/1916
Miscellaneous			
Miscellaneous	A Form. Messages And Signals.		
Miscellaneous	C Form (Original). Messages And Signals.	09/11/1916	09/11/1916
Miscellaneous	Deputy Director of Remounts.	08/03/1916	08/03/1916
Miscellaneous	87th Brigade. Divisional Artillery.	09/03/1916	09/03/1916
Miscellaneous	The General Officer Commanding, 9th Army Corps.	08/03/1916	08/03/1916
Miscellaneous	Allotment Of Berthing Accomodation		
Miscellaneous	Paras. 3 to 9 referred to in Para 4 of C.R. 15584/Q/5		
Miscellaneous	Appx 9 1-4		
Miscellaneous	The General Officer Commanding, 9th Corps, Suez. Appendix 9	09/03/1916	09/03/1916
Miscellaneous	87th Brigade. C.R.E.	10/03/1916	10/03/1916
Miscellaneous	The General Officer Commanding, 9th Corps, Suez.	09/03/1916	09/03/1916
Miscellaneous	A Form. Messages And Signals.		
Miscellaneous	C Form (Duplicate). Messages And Signals.	20/11/1916	20/11/1916
Miscellaneous	General Officer Commanding, 9th Corps, Suez.	10/03/1916	10/03/1916
Miscellaneous	Allotment Of Berthing Accomodation		
Miscellaneous	Telephone Message From 9th Corps	11/03/1916	11/03/1916
Miscellaneous	Officer i/c Signal. C.R.E. 86th Brigade. Camp Commandant. 88th Brigade.	11/03/1916	11/03/1916
Miscellaneous	Allotment Of Berthing Accomodation		
Miscellaneous	The General Officer Commanding, 9th Corps.	10/03/1916	10/03/1916
Miscellaneous	86th & 88th Brigades. C.R.E.	11/03/1916	11/03/1916
Miscellaneous	Train Allotment		
Miscellaneous	Train Timings	11/03/1916	11/03/1916
Miscellaneous	Appx 10 1-3		
Miscellaneous	87th Field Ambu R.A.M.C. 29th Division No 87	11/03/1916	11/03/1916
Miscellaneous	Programme of Training for week ending Saturday 11th March 1916	11/03/1916	11/03/1916
Miscellaneous	29th Division Appendix 10	11/02/1913	11/02/1913
Miscellaneous	4th Worcestershire Regiment	18/03/1916	18/03/1916

Miscellaneous	2/Bn. Hampshire Regiment Programme of Work Week Ending 18th March 1916		
Miscellaneous	Programme of Work for Week ending 18th March 1916	10/03/1916	10/03/1916
Miscellaneous	Programme of Work Week Ending	11/03/1916	11/03/1916
Miscellaneous	Programme of Work Newfoundland Regt.		
Miscellaneous	88th Machine Gun Company Programme of Work for week ending Saturday 18th March 1916.	10/03/1916	10/03/1916
Miscellaneous	29th Division Tactical Exercise.		
Map	Sketch To Illustrate Tactical Exercise on 10th March.		
Operation(al) Order(s)	29th Divisional Order No. 100.	11/03/1916	11/03/1916
Miscellaneous	C.R.E. C.R.A. 86th & 88th Brigades. Cyclists.	08/03/1916	08/03/1916
Miscellaneous	A Form. Messages And Signals.		
Miscellaneous	C Form (Duplicate). Messages And Signals.	11/11/1916	11/11/1916
Miscellaneous	Appx 11 1-4		
Miscellaneous	29th Division. Appendix 11	12/03/1916	12/03/1916
Miscellaneous			
Miscellaneous	C.R.A. A.D.M.S. Camp Commandant.	12/03/1916	12/03/1916
Miscellaneous	C Form (Duplicate). Messages And Signals.	12/11/1916	12/11/1916
Miscellaneous	The General Officer Commanding, 9th Corps. Suez.	11/03/1916	11/03/1916
Miscellaneous	Move of 2nd. Flight. 29th Division. 13th March Allotment of Berthing Accommodation		
Miscellaneous	A Form. Messages And Signals.		
Miscellaneous	C Form (Duplicate). Messages And Signals.	12/11/1916	12/11/1916
Miscellaneous	C Form (Original). Messages And Signals.	11/11/1916	11/11/1916
Miscellaneous	A Form. Messages And Signals.		
Miscellaneous	D.D.M.S., 9th. Corps.	10/03/1916	10/03/1916
Miscellaneous	29th Division.	12/03/1916	12/03/1916
Miscellaneous	A Form. Messages And Signals.		
Miscellaneous	Appx 12 1-3		
Miscellaneous	General Officer Commanding, 9th Corps, Suez. Appendix 12	12/03/1916	12/03/1916
Miscellaneous	Allotment Of Berthing Accommodation	15/03/1916	15/03/1916
Miscellaneous	Train Timings for The Move of 3rd Flight 29th Division on 14/15th March		
Miscellaneous	3rd Flight 29th Division		
Miscellaneous	Headqrs 88th Brigade.	13/03/1916	13/03/1916
Miscellaneous	Allotment Of Berthing Accommodation		
Miscellaneous	Train Timings for The Move of 3rd Flight 29th Division on 14/15th March		
Miscellaneous	3rd Flight 24th Division		
Miscellaneous	Wire has been received from Daglock Cairo as follow.	13/03/1916	13/03/1916
Miscellaneous	Appx 13 1-6		
Miscellaneous	2nd & 3rd Flights 29th Division. Appendix 13	12/03/1916	12/03/1916
Miscellaneous	2nd Flight. 29th Division		
Miscellaneous	Third Flight 29th Division.		
Miscellaneous	The following telephone message has been received from A.Q.M.G. Cairo this morning.	13/03/1916	13/03/1916
Miscellaneous	General Officer Commanding, 9th Corps Suez.	13/03/1916	13/03/1916
Miscellaneous	The General Officer Commanding, 9th Corps Suez.	13/03/1916	13/03/1916
Miscellaneous	To Headqrs 88th Bde	13/03/1916	13/03/1916
Miscellaneous	Allotment Of Berthing Accommodation		
Miscellaneous	To O.C. 16th Sanitary Section	16/03/1916	16/03/1916
Miscellaneous	Allotment Of Berthing Accommodation		
Miscellaneous	A Form. Messages And Signals.		
Miscellaneous			
Miscellaneous	Appx 14		

Miscellaneous	Billets 29th. Division. Appendix 14		
Operation(al) Order(s)	VIII Corps Operation Order No. 2	26/03/1916	26/03/1916
Miscellaneous	29th Division		
Miscellaneous	Appx 15		
Operation(al) Order(s)	Operation Order No. 23 by Major General H. de B. de Lisle, C.B., D.S.O. Commanding 29th Division.	28/03/1916	28/03/1916
Miscellaneous	29th Division		
Miscellaneous	March Table For March 30th 1918 Table "A"		
Miscellaneous	Appx 16		
Operation(al) Order(s)	Operation Order No. 24 by Major General H. de B. de Lisle C.B. D.S.O. Commanding 29th Division Appendix 16	30/03/1916	30/03/1916

20TH DIVISION

WO 95/2280

GENERAL STAFF
MAR - AUG 1916

20TH DIVISION

WO 95/2280

Arrived MARSEILLES from EGYPT 20th March 1916.

GENERAL STAFF

29th DIVISION

MARCH 1 9 1 6

Appendices attached :- 1 to 16 with sub files.
Appendices for February 1916 are also attached.

Confidential

Duplicate

War Diary

General Staff

29th Division

For the month of

March 1916.

Volume XIII

Confidential

Instructions regarding War Diaries and Intelligence Summaries are contained in F.S. Regs., Part II. and the Staff Manual respectively. Title pages will be prepared in manuscript.

WAR DIARY — GENERAL STAFF . 29TH DIVISION.

or

INTELLIGENCE SUMMARY
(Erase heading not required.)

Army Form C. 2118.

Place	Date	Hour	Summary of Events and Information	Remarks and references to Appendices
916.	1st March.		Marseilles) (1) 1 Officer Divisional Staff (A.A. & Q.M.G.) was detained by telegram at Q.M.G.) 3 officers from Division for entraining purposes, 6 subalterns as A.M.L.Os for entrainment and billeting duties. 1 Staff Officer from Q Branch Divisional Staff (D.A.A. & Q.M.G.) 1 Staff Officer from each Infantry Brigade, 1 Staff Officer Divisional Artillery, S.S.O. of Division, D.A.D.O.S. and D.A.D.M.S. left SUEZ by 1739 train. (App.) Notification received that (App) 1 Squadron Surrey Yeomanry (29th Division Squadron) would embark at Alexandria, and not join 29th Division here. (App. ———→).	App 1
			Captain Baldwin took over command of Divisional Cyclist Company. Headquarters 88th Brigade and Headquarters 87th Brigade returned to Suez Camp from SHALLUFA and KUBRI respectively. 15th Brigade R.H.A. and 17th Brigade R.F.A. moved from EL SHATT and AYUN MUSSA respectively to Suez Camp. (Vide Feb. App.)	
			February Appendices comprise:-	
			(1) G.S.26 dated 4th Feb.,1918 asking for reports from Units on proposed method of training specialists. Reports are attached.	
			(2) 9th Corps Q.362 forwarding copy of G.R.15478/Q stating that the 90th Heavy, 14th & 48th Siege Batteries and 2 Batteries 57th Brigade R.F.A., have orders to move to Suez from Alexandria.	1st App
			(3) 29th Division Order No. 21 re-move removal of Division to FRANCE.	
			(4) C.M.Q.445 from D.Q.M.G., M.E.F., giving instructions re embarkation 29th Division with amendment to para 5.	
			(5) G.A.216 reference Machine Gun Companies being separate Units.	
			(6) G.539 notifying 3rd Echelon that 29th Division Section is to be ready to embark	
			(7) G.537 same notification to Base Depot, Alexandria. Receipt attached.	
			(8) Q.N.742 re charges and ammunition to be taken. Information sent into Brigades: D.A.D.O.S. in G.569.	
			(9) I.G.C. Lev: Base. Instructions re flights for embarkation of 29th Division.	
			(10) A.461/3 in answer to above giving proposed flights.	
			(11) Q.N.849 from 9th Corps stating that Brigades R.A. will be made up to 4 Batteries on/	

WAR DIARY – GENERAL STAFF 29TH DIVISION.
or
INTELLIGENCE SUMMARY.
(Erase heading not required.)

Army Form C. 2118.

Instructions regarding War Diaries and Intelligence Summaries are contained in F.S. Regs., Part II. and the Staff Manual respectively. Title pages will be prepared in manuscript.

Place	Date	Hour	Summary of Events and Information	Remarks and references to Appendices
	1st March		on arrival in FRANCE.	
		12.	10th Indian Division Operation Order No: 17 reference move of Units of 29th Division from East of Canal to Suez.	
			March Appendix/comprises :-	
			(1) Statement of Officers to proceed as advanced party on LLANDOVERY CASTLE.	
			(2) C.R. 15584/Q/Q from I.G.C. reference embarkation of Surrey Yeomanry.	
			(3) G.576 to C.R.E. and D.M.D.O.S. re ammunition to be taken by R.E.	
			(4) C.M.Q.T.1835 cipher message re Cable section accompanying 29th Division, also G.A.232 and Q.N.453 referring to same thing.	Appx
			(5) Q.N.798 from 9th Corps reference advance party of 57th Howitzer Brigade and G.604 referring to same thing.	
			(6) 1530 from Div: R.A. giving marching out state of 460th Battery.	
			(7) S.C.1230 from 87th Brigade reference advance early party personnel of Machine Gun Co:	
			(8) G.595 to 9th Corps giving number of advance party of Artillery less 460th Battery.	
			(9) A/461/4 to 9th Corps list showing Officers and O.R. proceeding with advance party.	
			(10) A.D.O.S.150 9th Corps reference tents and Ordnance stores	
			(11) Q.N.762 from 9th Corps reference disposal of surplus vehicles and animals and G.A.231 to Units reference same subject attached.	
			(12) List of Officers and servants who embarked on LLANDOVERY CASTLE at PORT SAID on March 2nd.	

Army Form C. 2118.

WAR DIARY — GENERAL STAFF. 29TH DIVISION.
or
INTELLIGENCE SUMMARY
(Erase heading not required.)

Instructions regarding War Diaries and Intelligence Summaries are contained in F.S. Regs., Part II. and the Staff Manual respectively. Title pages will be prepared in manuscript.

Place	Date	Hour	Summary of Events and Information	Remarks and references to Appendices
	2nd March		460th Howitzer Battery proceeded to Alexandria to join 57th Howitzer Brigade. They took 44 horses. (App. 1.)	
			The full establishment of bicycles arrived, and were distributed. The Lewis Guns also arrived. (App.)	
			2 Battalions 86th Brigade (Lancs. Fus: and Munster Fus:) returned to Suez Camp from EL KUBRI.	
			A party of 8 officers and 57 Other Ranks of Supply Section, Divisional Train left for Alexandria at 1730 to embark on "NESTRIAN" and "CESTRIAN" also the following officers, 1 Senior Officer and 1 Transport Officer from 86th and 87th Brigades and 1 Senior Officer and 2 Transport Officers fromm 88th Brigade. All officers were accompanied by their servants. Total party proceeding = 15 officers, 64 Other Ranks. This party was redirected to PORT SAID to embark on "MANITOU" (Vide App.2)	App. 2
			March Appendix 2 comprises:- (1) Letter to 9th Corps stating officer to proceed to Alexandria to make up balances required on CESTRIAN and NESTRIAN, into amplified form of above dated 2nd March attached (2) Translation of Cipher Message from Daglock to 9th Corps reference accomodation in above 2 ships.	App.2
	3rd March		70 Officers and 136 Other Ranks Surrey Yeomanry/left Alexandria on "NESSIAN" Squadron (Vide App. 2)	
			March Appendix no. 3 comprises:- (1) Copy No. 21 Force order No. 12 reference new designation of 57th Howitzer Battery, now to be the 132nd F.A.H. Battery. (2) G.549 to 9th Corps asking for Captain Fraser and 35 O.R. for 29th Division Ammunition Section: attached are B.M.303 and G.606 referring to same matter. (3) C.R.15584/Q/1 from I.G.C. reference embarkation of advance parties on H.T.MANITOU with allotment and Berthing accomodation attached also detail of officers and O.R. of 1st Line Transport. (4)/	App. 3

T.2134. Wt. W708—776. 500000. 4/15. Sir J.C. & S.

WAR DIARY - GENERAL STAFF - 29TH DIVISION.

Army Form C. 2118.

Place	Date	Hour	Summary of Events and Information	Remarks and references to Appendices
	3rd March		(4) G.A.240 to Units notifying arrival of Lewis Guns with D.S.335 attached stating ammunition to be taken. (5) C.G.S.15 reference disposal of excess gun ammunition.	App. 3
	4th March		MANITOU 1st line personnel 9 Officers 815 Other Ranks left for PORT SAID to embark on (App. ——) orders for embarkation and instructions issued, see App. 3. The G.O.C.,A.D.C.,AWD.M.S, 2 A.D.Cs, G.S.O.3 and Signalling Officer returned from leave to England, also some other 20 Officers belonging to the Division, including Brigadier-General Cayley, Commanding 88th Brigade. March Appendix No. 4 comprises:- (1) O.S. 352 from A.D.O.SM. 9th Corps re gun ammunition to be taken. (2) O.S.361 reference S.A.A. to be taken with batteries R.F.A. and 15th Battery R.H.A. (3) B.M.409 from 29th D.A. acknowledging above.	App 4

Army Form C. 2118.

1916.

Instructions regarding War Diaries and Intelligence Summaries are contained in F.S. Regs., Part II. and the Staff Manual respectively. Title pages will be prepared in manuscript.

WAR DIARY - GENERAL STAFF 29th Division.
or
INTELLIGENCE SUMMARY.

(Erase heading not required.)

Place	Date	Hour	Summary of Events and Information	Remarks and references to Appendices
	5th March.		The 3 Sections 89th Field Ambulance East Bank of the Canal returned to SUEZ CAMP. "B" Section from AYUN MUSSA, and "A" and "C" Sections from KUBRI. 48th Siege Battery detrained in the morning at SUEZ Camp, and camped in the Artillery Camp there. (Feb. App.)	(Feb. App.)
	6th March.		Secret instructions were received from Corps that the 17th Brigade R.F.A., the 15th Bde. R.H.A., part of the 2/S.W.Bs would embark at Alexandria on March 8th on H.M.T.KINGSTONIAN and HUANCHACO. (vide App. 5.) Instructions were received later that owing to a mechanical breakdown on the Kingstonian this move was postponed for 24 hours (vide App.6.) From Order No. 12 issued by G.H.Q. was received from 9th Corps.(vide App.3) March Appendix 5 comprises:- (1) Copy of Memo. from A.Q.M.G. Cairo stating troops to be embarked on Kingstonian and Huanchaco with C.G.S.12 of 6th March passing on information and asking for number of chargers to be embarked, attached. (2) Marching out State of March 6th 1916. (3) List of Officers and Other Ranks who embarked on H.T. MANITO on March 5th at Port Said. H.T. MANITO on March 6th 1916.	(App.5) (App.6) (App.3)

Army Form C. 2118.

WAR DIARY — GENERAL STAFF 29th DIVISION.
or
INTELLIGENCE SUMMARY.
(Erase heading not required.)

Instructions regarding War Diaries and Intelligence Summaries are contained in F.S. Regs., Part II. and the Staff Manual respectively. Title pages will be prepared in manuscript.

1916.

Place	Date	Hour	Summary of Events and Information	Remarks and references to Appendices
	7th March.		G.O.C. inspected 86th Brigade at ceremonial parade. March Appendix 6 comprises:- (1) C.R.M. 15584/Q/3 -6/3/16, G.R.15584/Q/3 Table 2, C.R.15584/Q/3 -6/3/16, C.R./15584/Q/3 -7/3/16, C.R.15584/Q/3&4 (Train allotment No.1) C.R.15584/Q/3 (Train Timing No.1) Referring to embarkation of troops on H.T.KINGSTONIAN and H.T.CHUANCHACO giving train timings and allotments with figures amended to suit present strengths. (2) 29th Division Operation Order No.22 ref. embarkation on KINGSTONIAN & CHUANCHACO, with allotment of berthing accomodation with amendments to figures attached. (3) 15584/Q/4 from I.G.C. ref. embarkation on H.T.KAROA with allotment of berthing accomodation attached. (4) Q.500 statement of composition of a cavalry train, from 9th Corps.	
	8th March.		G.O.C. inspected 88th Brigade at a ceremonial parade. Orders received from 9th Corps for remainder of S.W.Bs to embark on 9th on transport H.T. KAROA, from Alexandria. (App.6) 14th Siege Battery detrained in the morning, and camped in Artillery Camp, Suez Camp. (Feb. Appendix) March Appendix 7 comprises:- (1) A.B.472 asking A.Q.M.G. Cairo, for extra accomodation on H.T.Karoa for 100 men caused by draft to C.R.A. The following messages are attached with reference to the same thing, 4484 from Daglock, Q.N.888 from 9th Corps, A.B.473, A.BN474. (2) Orders to 87th Brigade reference embarkation of S.W.Bs on H.T.KAROA with allotment of berthing accomodation and a copy of train allotments and timings to all concerned giving figures as amended in pencil in Appendix 6.	(App.4.) (Feb.App.)

1916.

WAR DIARY - GENERAL STAFF 29th DIVISION.
or
INTELLIGENCE SUMMARY.

Army Form C. 2118.

Instructions regarding War Diaries and Intelligence Summaries are contained in F.S. Regs., Part II. and the Staff Manual respectively. Title pages will be prepared in manuscript.

(Erase heading not required.)

Place	Date	Hour	Summary of Events and Information	Remarks and references to Appendices
	9th March.		On the night of the 8/9th 15th Bde. R.H.A. 17th Bde R.F.A., 2/S.W.Bs, and a few Officers' chargers entrained for Alexandria for embarkation on the KINGSTONIAN and HUANCHACO, and KAROA (vide App.6).	(App.6) (Feb. Ap
			90th Heavy Battery detrained in the morning and camped in Suez Camp. (Feb. App.) Orders were received for move of the Inniskilling K.O.S.Bs, 147th Bde. R.F.A. and a portion of the 57th How. Bde. on 10th and 11th. (App.8)	(App.8)
			March Appendix 8 comprises:-	
			(1) C.R.15584/Q/5 from I.G.S. giving orders for 1st Flight of Division to embark on the H.T. MEGANTIC, ELELE, Wandilla, allotment of berthing accomodation and train allotment and timings are attached.	App 8.
			(2) Summary of a cypher wire No. 4490 dated 8/3/16 stating troops to embark on H.T. Wandilla and MEGANTIC.	
			(3) A.B.479 to G.O.C. Alexandria. ref. orders to 57th Bde. (How.) and answer attached.	
			(4) Memo from A.Q.M.G. Cairo. ref. entraining of 326 horses from ABBASSIA for the H.T.KAROA from Alexandria.	
			(5) Copy of Memo. sent from 29th Division to all concerned ref. embarkation H.T. MEGANTIC ELELE, and WANDILLA, with copy of allotment of berthing accomodation attached.	
	10th March.		G-in-C inspected 1st Royal Inniskilling Fusiliers, of which Regt. he is Colonel. The 147th Bd. R.F.A. and Headquarters 87th Bde. with ½ the K.O.S.Bs entrained during the evening for embarkation on the H.T.ELELE and H.T. MEGANTIC respectively, the former at Alexandria the latter at Port Said. The remainder K.O.S.Bs and 1st Royal Inniskilling Fusiliers embarked on the H.T.WANDILLA at Suez Docks during the after-noon ; also a portion of the 87th Bde. Machine Gun Coy. (embarkation instruction are attached, vide App.8)	(App.8)
			March Appendix 9 comprise:-	
			(1) C.R.15584/4/6 from I.G.C. ref. embarkation of troops on H.T.WARILDA and allotment of berthing accomodation attached.	App 9
			(2) O.G.G.S.12 copy of above order sent to all concerned and note as to chargers applied for to complete.	

WAR DIARY – GENERAL STAFF – 29TH DIVISION.

INTELLIGENCE SUMMARY.

Army Form C. 2118.

1916.

Place	Date	Hour	Summary of Events and Information	Remarks and references to Appendices
	10th March		March Appendix 9 contd.	
			(3) A.B.493 to all concerned as above, ref. arrangements for embarkation, timings, transport, etc., with embarkation officers 37/1 giving instructions in this matter attached.	App. 9
			(4) C.R.15584/Q/7 from I.G.C. ref. embarkation on H.T. MENOMINEE at Alexandria, allotment of berthing accomodation and telephone from 9th Corps are attached. Also Divisional Orders to all concerned, train timings No.3 and Divisional Order giving train allotment and train timing.	
	11th March		A tactical exercise was carried out during the morning, Brigadier General Williams commanded the Division in an attack on BIR SUEZ from the West. (The scheme toge her with the Directors' remarks is attached to appendix 10.	(App. 10)
			The Border Regt., 88th Field Ambulance, remainder of the 87th Brigade Machine Gun Company, 1/2nd London Company R.E., and Mobile Vet. Section embarked at Suez Docks on the WARILDA during the morning. (App.9). The Roy Dublin Fus; R.E. Headquarters, remainder of Divisional horses, and the 29th Divisional Section entrained during the evening in two trains for embarkation on the MENOMINEE at Alexandria on 12th March. (App.)	(Appx 9) (App. 9)
			March appendix 10 comprises:-	App. 10
			(1) Programme of work of all Units for week ending March 18th.	
			(2) General and Special Idea for 29th Division Tactical Exercise with sketch, 29th Divisional Order 100, and Special Order attached.	
			(3) A.B.497 to G.O.C. Alexandria District ref. orders for 147th Brigade R.F.A. and Artillery reinforcements, and reply attached.	

Army Form C. 2118.

WAR DIARY—GENERAL STAFF 29th DIVISION.

or

INTELLIGENCE SUMMARY.

(Erase heading not required.)

Instructions regarding War Diaries and Intelligence
Summaries are contained in F.S. Regs, Part II.
and the Staff Manual respectively. Title pages
will be prepared in manuscript.

1916.

Place	Date	Hour	Summary of Events and Information	Remarks and references to Appendices
	12th March.		16 Officers and 209 Other Ranks and 250 Horses 147th Bde. R.F.A. embarked in MENOMINEE at Alexandria having spent the night in Rest Camp at Alexandria. (App.)	(App. 9)
			March Appendix 11 comprises:-	
			(1) 9th Corps Memo giving instructions for embarkation on H.T. MILTIADES on 13th March with 29th Division Order on the subject to all concerned, also instructions from embarkation Officer attached.	
			(2) G.R.15584/Q/8 from I.G.C. ref. embarkation on H.T. MILTIADES with allotment of berthing accomodation attached.	App 11
			(3) The following messages referring to the embarkation of the 189 Officers' chargers required to complete establishment and as regards the necessary personnel to look after them:- G.A.245, A.H.499, A.B.500, A.B.501, N.R.104,4521, A.B.504.	
			(4) D.D.M.S.494 ref. No. 16 Sanitary Section being attached to the 29th Divn., Q.544 & G.664 referring to same matter are attached.	
	13th March.		The following embarked on H.T.MILTIADES at SUEZ during the morning(App. 11) Divisional Headquarters(less GS,O.2 and A.P.M.) Royal Artillery Hd.Qrs., 1st West Riding Coy. R.E. 87th Field Ambce., 1st Lancs. Fusiliers, 86th Bde Headquarters, Divisional Band. Total 67 Officers, 1250 Other Ranks.	(App. 11)
			Captain GEE Royal Fusiliers assumed duties of Staff Capt. 86th Bde. vice Capt EDLUNDH who rejoined his regt.	
			Lieut Colonel BISHOP and LIEUT. COLONEL RICE handed over command of the Lancs .Fusrs. and Worcester Regt. respectively to the next senior officer and were ordered to proceed to England.	
			March Appendix 12 comprises:-	
			(1) G.R.15584/Q/9 from I.G.C. giving instructions for embarkation of troops on H.T.TRANSYLVANIA on 15th March, with allotment of berthing accomodation (Table N0.8)	App 12

Army Form C. 2118.

WAR DIARY - GENERAL STAFF.
or
INTELLIGENCE SUMMARY

(Erase heading not required.)

Instructions regarding War Diaries and Intelligence Summaries are contained in F.S. Regs., Part II. and the Staff Manual respectively. Title pages will be prepared in manuscript.

1916.

Place	Date	Hour	Summary of Events and Information	Remarks and references to Appendices
	13th March.		March Appendix 12 Contd. (1) contd. train timings No.4 and train allotments No.4 attached. (2) Divisional Orders on above embarkation, copies of the same documents being attached with figures amended accordingly to latest strengths. (3) Wire from Daglock stating that H.T.ALAUNIA can carry extra troops, and that 1/5th R.Scots will proceed by that ship and not the LAKE MANITOBA.	App 12
	14th March.		The following embarked on H.T.ALAUNIA at SUEZ during the morning, 2/R.Fusrs., 1st R.Munster Fusiliers, West Kent Field Coy. R.E., NFLD Battalion, 1/5th R.Scots, 1 Chaplain, total 110 Officers 2227 Other Ranks. (App.) The following left by train from Suez Camp during the night 14/15th March for embarkation on the TRANSYLVANIA at Alexandria:- 88th Bde. Machine Gun Coy. 88th Bde. HdQrs., 4th Worcester Regt, 2nd Hants Regt., 1st Essex Regt. Total 102 Officers 2902 Other Ranks. (App.) March Appendix 13 consists comprising:- (1) C.R.15584/Q/10 from I.G.C. giving instructions ref. embarkation on H.T.ALAUNIA and H.T. LAKE MANITOBA with berthing accomodation attached also Q.453 ref. times of sailing. (2) C.R.15584/Q/11 from I.G.C. ref. extra accomodation on H.T.ALAUNIA. (3) C.R.15584/Q/12 confirming time of sailing of above ships. (4) Divisional Orders re embarkation on H.T.ALAUNIA and allotment of berthing accomodation. (5) Divisional Orders as above in case of LAKE MANITOBA with detailed instructions attached (A.B.534.) (6) List of ships on which the 29th Division embarked for France, giving rough numbers of Officers, Other Ranks, and horses on each ship. H.M.T. MILTIADES with Division Headquarters arrived at PORT SAID at 6.30 a.m. and sailed at 10 p.m.	(App.12) (App 13) App 13

Army Form C. 2118.

WAR DIARY - GENERAL STAFF 29th Division.

INTELLIGENCE SUMMARY

(Erase heading not required.)

Instructions regarding War Diaries and Intelligence Summaries are contained in F.S. Regs., Part II. and the Staff Manual respectively. Title pages will be prepared in manuscript.

Place	Date	Hour	Summary of Events and Information	Remarks and references to Appendices
	1916. 16th March.		The following embarked on H.T. LAKE MANITOBA at SUEZ. 29th Divisional Headquarters 2 Officers and 3 Other Ranks, 86th Brigade Machine Gun Company, 9 Officers 108 Other Ranks, Cyclists, 2 Officers 207 Other Ranks, 89th Field Ambulance 10 Officers 224 Other Ranks, Signal Company 2 Officers 35 Other Ranks, 16th Sanitary Section 1 Officer 37 Other Ranks, 2nd S.W.Bs. 1 Other Rank, 1st K.O.S.Bs 1 Other Rank, 13th Battery R.F.A. 1 Other Rank. Total 26 Officers 614 Other Ranks. The ship sailed at 4.30 p.m. (vide App./3)	App/3
	18th March.		The following details of 29th Division from Alexandria Base Depot joined the H.T. MANITOBA at PORT SAID:- 15th Brigade R.H.A.; 47th Other Ranks, Surrey Yeomanry 7 Other Ranks, 29th Division Ammunition Park R.F.A. 23 Other Ranks, 29th Divisional Ammunition Column 8 Other Ranks, 1st Essex Regiment 92 Other Ranks, 4th Worcester Regt. 4 Officers 63 Other Ranks, 1/5th Royal Scots 1 Officer 20 Other Ranks, 2nd Hants. 82 Other Ranks, Newfoundland Regt. 45 Other Ranks, 1/2 London Field Company R.E. 8 Other Ranks, 1st West Riding Company R.E. 4 Other Ranks, 1st Royal Dublin Fusiliers 2 Officers 1 Other Rank, Royal Inniskilling Fusiliers 2 Officers 2 Other Ranks, Records Section 2 Officers 29 Other Ranks, 3/1st London Divisional Signal Company 1 Officer 28 Other Ranks. Total 12 Officers 459 Other Ranks. Grand total on board H.T. MANITOBA 38 Officers 1073 Other Ranks.	

Army Form C. 2118.

1916.

Instructions regarding War Diaries and Intelligence Summaries are contained in F. S. Regs., Part II. and the Staff Manual respectively. Title pages will be prepared in manuscript.

WAR DIARY - 29th DIVISION. GENERAL STAFF.

or

~~INTELLIGENCE SUMMARY.~~

(Erase heading not required.)

Place	Date	Hour	Summary of Events and Information	Remarks and references to Appendices
	19th March		H.T. MANITOBA sailed from Port Said 7.p.m.	
	20th March		H.M.T. MILTIADES arrived at MARSEILLES at 8 a.m. G.O.C. and Divisional Headquarters Staff left MARSEILLES by mail train at 7.5 p.m. D.A.A. & Q.M.G. met ship on arrival, and supervised disembarkation and entrainment. Remainder of Divisional Headquarters proceeded by troop train.	
	21st March		Divisional Headquarters established at Long. G.O.C. and Divisional Headquarters arrived at LONG, some 10 Miles S.E. of ABBEVILLE, and took up their quarters in the Chateau there. A.A. & Q.M.G. had been at PONT REMY near ABBEVILLE for some days, and had made all arrangements for billeting the Division. He met Divisional Headquarters on arrival.	

T2134. Wt. W708-776. 500000. 4/15. Sir J. C. & S.

Army Form C. 2118.

WAR DIARY – GENERAL STAFF 29th DIVISION.
INTELLIGENCE SUMMARY

(Erase heading not required.)

Instructions regarding War Diaries and Intelligence Summaries are contained in F. S. Regs., Part II. and the Staff Manual respectively. Title pages will be prepared in manuscript.

1916.

Place	Date	Hour	Summary of Events and Information	Remarks and references to Appendices.
	26th March.		H.T. MANITOBA arrived Marseilles, the whole of the 29th Division having now been transferred to France. Except some B ase Details still to come from Alexandria. VIII Corps Operation Order No.2 reference limits of trench to be occupied by the Division etc. is attached as Appendix 14	(App. 14A)
	29th March.		The last troops of the 29th Division arrived in the new billeting area about 10 miles South of ABBEVILLE.(for allotment of billets vide app.14) Lord Kitchener visited General de Lisle at Long during the afternoon. March Appendix No.14 comprises:- (1) Billets of 29th Division. (2) 8th Corps operation order No.2 with the table of suggested billets and accomodation of village attached.	(App. 14)

T2134. Wt. W708 –776. 500000. 4/15. Sir J.C. & S.

WAR DIARY – GENERAL STAFF 29th DIVISION.

or

INTELLIGENCE SUMMARY.

(Erase heading not required.)

Army Form C. 2118.

1916.

Instructions regarding War Diaries and Intelligence Summaries are contained in F.S. Regs., Part II. and the Staff Manual respectively. Title pages will be prepared in manuscript.

Place	Date	Hour	Summary of Events and Information	Remarks and references to Appendices
	30th March		87th Brigade, West Riding Field Company R.E., 87th Field Ambulance moved from DOMART to new billets in AMPLIER also No.2 Company A.S.C. (vide Operation Order 23 App.13)	(App.13)
	31st March		The 86th Brigade, Kent Field Company R.E. and 89th Field Ambulance moved to billets at BEAUVAL and CANDAS, the Surrey Yeomanry So HEM, Divisional HQ and RE Headquarters and Mobile Vet. Section to BEAUQUESNE. No 2. Company A.S.C. moved to BEAUVAL. (vide Operation Order No.24.App.14) Headquarters and the 4 Brigades of Artillery moved to DOMART.	(App.14)

(Sgd) C.E.?
for G.O.C. ?

Appendices for

February 1916

"A" Form. Army Form C. 2121.
MESSAGES AND SIGNALS.

TO: 29th D.A.

Sender's Number	Day of Month	In reply to Number	AAA
DL 1	31st		

The following points should receive your attention during the training of your brigades.

1. The regulation pace at a trot is usually exceeded by artillery transport as well as by individuals, and the attention of all ranks must be called to this.

2. All batteries must be taught that except for ranging purposes battery fire at regular intervals is valueless and the only really effective fire is obtained by gun fire or section fire. The criticism that gun fire is expensive in ammunition is not just because one round gun fire a minute expends identically the same ammunition as battery fire 15 secs. but is far more effective morally as well as physically.

"A" Form.
MESSAGES AND SIGNALS.
Army Form C. 2121.

TO { Continued

3. Too much attention can be paid to all exercises that induce discipline such as Ceremonial dismounted, guard duties & even on occasions saluting parades. In all such it is advisable not to keep back small units and even individuals who have reached the required standard on account of others who for any cause fail to do so but it is most desirable that the divisional artillery should attain the same high standard which I expect from the remainder of the division and which has already been reached in some cases. At present I am not satisfied with the standard generally attained by the divisional artillery.

From G.O.C.
Place
Time 11.15

No. S 479

O.Cs All Units (1 copy to 29th Division).

The Brigade has now reached the stage when we must consider the training of Battalion "specialists" up to, and in some cases in excess, of establishments laid down in War Establishments Part VII.

These figures should be adhered to even in the case of Battalions at present below strength, ensuring that we have the necessary cadre to absorb the recruits, that the recruiting boom of November last is bound to produce in the near future.

The following list shows the men whom we may consider as specialists, their establishment, and the steps it is proposed to take in the Brigade for their training.

(a) Machine-gunners. 1 officer 27 rank and file (exclusive transport drivers). Battalions should have a sufficiency of trained gunners to replace 300% of casualties i.e. 3 trained sections.

- 2 -

It is proposed in the course of the next day or two, to group 2 officers and 2 sections per Battalion into one camp under direct control of Brigade Machine Gun Officer, this will it is hoped tend to greater uniformity of training throughout the Brigade.

(B) <u>Grenadiers</u>. 1 officer, 2 sergeants and 8 rank and file Battalion Hdqrs, 8 rank and file per Platoon.

At present little more than the selection of Battalion grenadier officers and N.C.O's can be done.

A Divisional Grenade School is to be formed, and a further memo: on the training and qualifications of grenadiers will be issued shortly.

(C) <u>Signallers</u>. Battalion Hdqrs. 16 rank and file Telephonists, 8 trained signallers per Company.

A telephone course of 8 men per Bn. is commencing on 7th inst, under the 29th Divisional Signal Coy.

(D) <u>Transport (side and drive)</u>. 1 officer, 1 sergeant, and 20 rank and file.

- 3 -

Further instructions will be issued on the arrival of vehicles and horses.

(e) <u>Stretcher Bearers</u>. 16 per Bn should receive thorough instructions in first aid etc, from the R.M.O.
This applies to BN. Sanitary Squads, (1 sergeant 10 men) also.

(f) <u>Battalion Snipers</u>. These will receive special training. Full instructions as to their duties, establishments etc. will be issued shortly.

3/2/16.

T.H. Gee   Captain.
for Bde Major 86th Bde
for Brig-Genl Cmdg 86 Bde

Officer i/c.,

    29th Divisional Cyclist Company.

    Please report what arrangements you propose to make for the training of the following "Specialists", which are included in the War Establishment of a Divisional Cyclist Company:-

    (i)   8 men trained in "first aid".

    (ii)   4 men trained in sanitary duties.

    (iii)   1 N.C.O. and 12 men trained signallers for communications.

    This is in addition to the training of the whole company as Grenadiers, arrangements for which are being made by the Divisional Grenadier Officer.

                            C.G. Fuller

                            Lieut Colonel, G.S.

4th February 1916.   29th Division.

II

G.S.O.
29a. Division

    I have sufficient men trained in the duties named above, but would like, if it could be arranged, for those trained under (i) & (ii) to be given a refresher course under a Medical Officer.

3.

A.D.M.S.

Please arrange for the necessary refresher course to be given to these men by one of the Medical Officers of the Division. Please return correspondence.

C. Fuller
Lt Col. G.S.

29: Divn H.Qrs
7-2-16.

4

To G.S.O. I

I have arranged for the course to be given by the M.O. i/c 29th Divn Cyclists who is also M.O. i/c R.E.

H. Wanton
Capt
D.A.D.M.S. 29 Divn

8-2-16

Officer i/c.,

29th Divisional Cyclist Company.

Please report what arrangements you propose to make for the training of the following "Specialists", which are included in the War Establishment of a Divisional Cyclist Company:-

    (i)   8 men trained in "first aid".

    (ii)   4 men trained in sanitary duties.

    (iii)   1 N.C.O. and 12 men trained signallers for communications.

This is in addition to the training of the whole company as Grenadiers, arrangements for which are being made by the Divisional Grenadier Officer.

4th February 1916.

                                            Lieut Colonel, G.S.
                                            29th Division.

3.

A.D.M.S.

Please arrange for the necessary refresher course to be given to these men by one of the Medical Officers of the Division. Please return correspondence.

C. Fuller
Lt.Col.
G.S.

29: Divn HdQrs
7-2-16.

4.

To G.S.O. I

I have arranged for this course to be given by the M.O. of 29th Divn Cyclists & also to M.O. of R.E.

H. H. Canton
Capt
D.A.D.M.S. 29 Divn

8-2-16

Officer i/c.,
    29th Divisional Cyclist Company.

       Please report what arrangements you propose to make for the training of the following "Specialists", which are included in the War Establishment of a Divisional Cyclist Company:-

    (i)   8 men trained in "first aid".

    (ii)   4 men trained in sanitary duties.

    (iii) 1 N.C.O. and 12 men trained signallers for communications.

       This is in addition to the training of the whole company as Grenadiers, arrangements for which are being made by the Divisional Grenadier Officer.

4th February 1916.

                                    Lieut Colonel, G.S.
                                        29th Division.

86th, 87th, and 88th Brigades.

With reference to G.S. Memorandum No.29 of the 1st February 1916, please furnish a short statement of the arrangements which you are making for the training of the undermentioned "Specialists":-

    (i) Machine Gunners.
   (ii) Grenadiers.
  (iii) Signallers.
   (iv) Transport Drivers.
    (v) Stretcher Bearers.
   (vi) Sanitary Squads.
 (vii) Battalion Snipers.

It is considered that the training of battalion snipers should be subservient to general field training and to the training of "Specialists" in other branches.

Lieut Colonel, G.S.
29th Division.

4th February 1916.

C.R.A.

C.R.E.

With Reference to G.S. Memorandum No.29 of the 1st February 1916, please furnish a short statement of the arrangements which you are making for the training of "Specialists", such as:-

        (i) Signallers and telephonists.
       (ii) Rangetakers.
      (iii) Look-out men.
      (iv) Medical Officer's orderlies.
      (v) Drivers.
     (vi) Sanitary Squads.

Lieut. Colonel, G.S.

29th Division.

4th February 1916.

86th Bde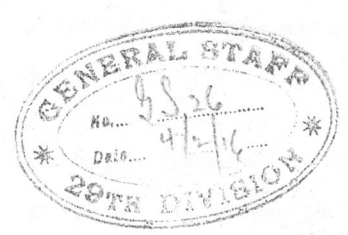

With reference to G.S.Memorandum No.29 of the 1st February 1916, please furnish a short statement of the arrangements which you are making for the training of the undermentioned "Specialists":-

(i) Machine Gunners.
(ii) Grenadiers.
(iii) Signallers.
(iv) Transport Drivers.
(v) Stretcher Bearers.
(vi) Sanitary Squads.
(vii) Battalion Snipers.

It is considered that the training of battalion snipers should be subservient to general field training and to the training of "Specialists" in other branches.

Your memo: S.479 answers all the above questions except N°: (vi).

G. Fuller

Lieut Colonel, G.S.
4th February 1916. 29th Division.

II

Sanitary Squads are being trained by Reg^{tl} M. O^s.

W. S. Williams
Brig Genl
Comdg 86th Inf Bde

4/2/16

B.603.
5.2.16.

The Staff Captain,
87th Infy Bde.

Reference your memo d/4.2.16 regarding training of Specialists:- the following arrangements are being made.

Machine Gunners & Signallers will be trained continually as units under the Machine Gun Officer and Signalling Sergeant respectively.

Grenadiers will be trained as a unit on the early morning parades only.

Stretcher Bearers will be trained in the handling of wounded and first aid by the Medical Officer as also will the sanitary squad.

Arrangements will be made for training Transport Drivers on arrival of 1st Line Transport.

Battalion snipers will be trained in the use of field glasses and telescopes and will be further trained during musketry. I should be glad if a telescopic rifle could be provided in order that they could be thoroughly instructed in its use.

W Clague Capt for Capt
Commdg 8th Bn The Border Regt

29th Division:

Ref G.S. 26. 4.12.16.—

Up to now, the training of specialists, with the exception of Machine Gunners, has received no attention, as it was considered advisable for these men to remain in the ranks with their companies for the time being, in order that they should reach a certain standard of excellence as regards drill etc before undergoing any advanced training as specialists.

In most cases this standard is now considered to have been attained, & during the coming week, Classes of instruction will be started both regimentally for the training of the junior NCOs & men & by the Brigade for the more senior NCOs & officers, both in machine gun work & in bombing. Stretcher bearers & Sanitary Squads will be trained regimentally under M.Os & Bn Snipers will be under the supervision of Bn Grenadier Officers.

It would be a great convenience if an officer from both the Signals & also from the A.S.C. might be detailed to instruct classes advanced classes both in Signalling & Transport duties.

Feb. 5th 1916.

J. A. Wilson Capt
for GOC 88th Bde

From O.C.
29th Div. Sig. Co. R.E.

To Lt. Col. Fuller
29th Division.

Progress report re
Instructional Class in Signal Duties.

I have the honour to report that a class consisting of 2 officers and 32 men sent by the Royal Munster Fusiliers assembled on the 7th inst. for instruction in signalling and signal duties.

The men attending the class have been (previously) classified as 1st class signallers and the work is therefore of an advanced nature; the following subjects have been dealt with:-

Buzzer practice.
Office routine and method of transmitting messages by telegraph & telephone.
Practical work on the above.
Elementary electrical theory (circuits &c) & construction of the field telephone.

It is intended to deal with the following subjects:-

Care & adjustment of the telephone.
Laying & maintenance of lines.
Methods of avoiding overhearing and interference and detecting & repairing faults.

(2)

1. Methods of instruction in Signal Duties
2. Organization of the Army Signal Service.

Attention is being paid to all available Standing & Routine Orders, Notes & Memos from D.A.S.K. on the subject.

L. Phillips Lt.
11/2/16. O.C. 39th Div. Sig. Co. R.E. T.

Time Table
for officers on course of instruction

Date.	Morning.	Afternoon.
Tuesday. 8/2/16.	9.30 to 10.30 Riding. 10.30 to 11.15 Construction of Saddlery etc. Saddlers Shop	2.15 - 3.30 Riding. Fitting of Saddlery & Harness of teams to receive special attention with Saddler in attendance to fit.
Wednesday 9/2/16	9.30 - 10.30 Riding. 10.30 - 11.15 Wheelers Shop Construction of Vehicles, Samples & parts Types of vehicles.	2.15 - 3.30. Riding Wheelers Shop.
Thursday 10/2/16.	9.20 - 10.30 Riding } Same as Wed. 10.30 - 11.15 }	Lecture by C.O. at time suitable to him - forage feeding shoeing & care of horses.
Friday 11/2/16	9.30 - 10.30 Riding 10.30 - 11.15 Farriers Shop.	2.15 - 3.30 Riding Farriers Shop. Lecture by V.O. at time suitable to him - Simple ailments and their treatment.
Saturday 12/2/16.	9.30 - 10.30. Riding 10.30 - 11.15 Farriers Shop.	2.15 - 3.30 Riding Farriers Shop
Sunday 13/2/16	9.30 - 10.30 Riding	Afternoon Clear.
Monday 14/2/16.	9.30 - 10.30 Riding 10.30 - 11.30 General instruction & questioning of class.	

Note:- In addition to above Officers attending Class will be present at all Stable hours (except Sunday Afternoon) During these hours Coy. Commanders will give them every assistance in acquiring knowledge of Stable routine, & either give them general instruction themselves or detail a good N.C.O. to do so.

Lt. Whittington to supervise riding, ride & drive & long reins; Lt. Horne other classes.

R.J. Mathews Capt. Adjt.

C.R.E.

29th Division.

With Reference to G.S.Memorandum No.29 of the 1st February 1916, please furnish a short statement of the arrangements which you are making for the training of "Specialists", such as:-

        (i) Signallers and telephonists.
       ~~(ii) Rangetakers.~~
      ~~(iii) Look-out men.~~
      (iv) Medical Officer's orderlies.
      (v) Drivers.
      (vi) Sanitary Squads.

                                    C.J. Fuller

                                Lieut. Colonel, G.S.

4th February 1916.   29th Division.

2

H.Q. 29th Div.

(i). I am endeavouring to arrange with O.C. Div'l Signal Coy for the training of 1 N.C.O. & 3 men per Coy (總 total 1 + 2 per Coy) in Semaphore & Morse (Lamp & Flag).

(iv). Until HQ Divl. RE are brought up to estbt I cannot provide medical orderlies, & cannot therefore train them.

(v). I am at present short of 85 drivers, & have no horses, (except 6 offrs chargers) harness, saddlery or vehicles.

As soon as sufficient drivers, horses (or mules), vehicles & harness arrive for any Coy, the O.C. of such Coy will arrange for the instruction of the drivers in:—

(a). Stable management.
(b). Riding & driving.
(c). Fitting of harness & saddlery.
(d). Shoeing (not the actual process but correct fitting of shoes).

As regards (a) a series of lectures on horsemastership has already been given, at which all officers & mounted NCOs attended.

(vii). These have already been formed, and are being instructed in their duties by the M.O. i/c Divl. RE.

5/2/15.

[signature] Lt Col
C.R.E.

27th Division

Attached reports for Training of Specialists forwarded.

Regarding the application of 1/ Border Regt for Telescopic Rifle, this can be supplied by me.

W. Sinclair Lockhart
Captain
Staff Capt for GOC 87th pde

5/5/16

HEADQUARTERS
No. B.603
Date 5/5/16
87th INFANTRY BRIGADE

Suez 5/2/16

Proposed Programme of Training
for Specialists

I Machine Gunners

Daily training under M.G. Officer in mechanism and firing of guns. On Bn Route March days M. Gunners accompany the Bn.

As soon as gun limbers arrive M.G. Section will do 3 days a week field work attached to Coys or Bn in tactical operations.

II Grenadiers

Three days a week training under Grenadier Officer (special trenches will be dug for this training). There are at present no bombs in the Bn. Grenadiers attend all route marches

III Signallers

Training daily under instructors in helio, lamp and flag. Signallers attend Bn Route Marches. After first week signallers will be attached to Coys or Bn for tactical operations.

IV Transport Drivers

As soon as 1st Line transport arrives it is proposed that half the drivers shall be new men to enable them to learn the management of horses, riding etc.

V. Stretcher Bearers

3 days a week instruction in first aid under the M.O. Attend all Route Marches.

VI. Sanitary Squads

Will be formed and go through short courses under the M.O.

VII. Battalion Snipers

It is proposed to start a class of about 20 men under a selected officer. These men will be trained to use the Telescopic sight; also to pick up positions to establish themselves in by day and night.

E. J. W. Byrne
Capt
for Major Commanding
2 S. Wales Bord.

Staff Capt.
87th Inf Bde.

Statement of arrangements for Training Specialists in 1st R. Inniskilling Fus.

(1). <u>Machine Gunners</u> — The M.G. officer, will have his 28 trained men and 17 men for classes, absolutely at his disposal during the next week.

(2) <u>Grenadiers</u>. I understood that Bns were to wait until the Brigade gave them grenades for practice or called for names for a school. I am doing nothing.

(3). The trained signallers not used as instructors are practising hard with the helio. A class of 14 men has been in training for the past 10 days. They attend no other parades & are making good progress.

4. <u>Transport Drivers</u>
5. <u>Stretcher Bearers</u>
6. <u>Sanitary Squads</u>
7. <u>Battalion Snipers</u>

} In none of these categories have I taken any steps nor do I propose to do so until later on in a week or fortnights time.

R C French Lt Col
1st Inniskillings

5/2/16.

To
Staff Captain
87th Infy Brigade

Reference your memo of yesterday's date the following is a short statement of how it is proposed to train the Specialists.

MACHINE GUNNERS

The Machine Gunners are being trained under the M.G. Officer in a course which includes the following: Description of parts, Mechanism, Gun drill with time test, Stoppages with time test, Target & Range practices, Care of guns, Range finding with instrument, Selection of positions and gun laying.

GRENADIERS

Arrangements will be made for the training of Grenadiers as soon as bombs & catapults are available.

SIGNALLERS

These will be instructed in Flag drill (Morse & Semaphore), Helios & Field Telephones, also Map reading, beginning on Monday 7th inst.

TRANSPORT DRIVERS

At present there is no opportunity for training these men as there is no transport personnel with the Battn.

STRETCHER BEARERS AND SANITARY SQUADS

These men will be trained by the Medical Officer of the Bn.

P.T.O

BATTALION SNIPERS.

Snipers will be selected during the progress of Battn Musketry Course and will be trained under supervision of an Officer on the lines laid down in the recent report on Sniping in Trench Warfare, as modified by recent experience in Gallipoli.

Sherwood-Kelly
Lt Colonel
Commdg 1st Bn R. Innis. Fus.

5/2/16

29th Division

Ref. your G.S. 26 7.2.16

1. Classes daily.
2. ditto.
3. ditto.
4. Practical instruction & lectures.
5. Riding & driving Drill
6. Practical instruction & lectures

29th Dn
BM/800)
8.2.16

CH Clark Major R.A.
Brigade Major 29th Dn
for Comdg 29th Dn

To/ GSO I
29th Div.

[Stamp: A.D.M.S. No. 91 Date 22-2-16 29TH DIVISION]

Reference your G.S. 34 of 7/2/16.
A course of Two Lectures has been given to the Medical Officers attached to Battalions in the Division. The lectures were of 3/4 hr duration, & the following points were thoroughly dealt with.
1. Duties of M.O.s & Battalions on Active Service
2. Personnel under M.O.
3. Responsibility of M.O, C.O. & Quartermaster to regard to Sanitation
4. Disposal of Sick & Unfit
5. Duties while Regt is in Action with practical illustrations from the Gallipoli campaign.

A.D.M.S.
No. 91
Date 22-2-16
29TH DIVISION

6. Sanitation in camp & trenches.
7. Training of Sanitary Squad, Stretcher Squad
8. Regimental etiquette.

The following Officers were present.

		21st	22nd
Lt Frew		✓	✓
Capt Sanders		✓	✓
Lt Wheeler	88th	✓	✓
" Nicholas	Bde	✓	✓
Capt Saw		✓	On Leave
" Whitaker		✓	✓
" Walsh	87th	✓	✓
Lt Wamsley	Bde	✓	✓
" Young		✓	✓
" Walker		✓	✓
Capt Harris	RA	✓	✓
Lt Hendrie		✓	✓
" Duffy	RE	✓	✓
" Allen	ASC	✓	✓

H T Panton
Capt
DADMS 29 Div.

C.R. 15478/Q

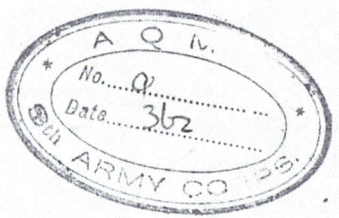

General Officer Commanding,

Alexandria District.

       Orders have been received from General Headquarters M.E.F. for the following moves from Alexandria to Suez :-

       90th Heavy Battery
       14th Siege Battery
       48th Siege Battery
       57th Brigade R.F.A. (2 batteries) These have no horses.

       Please arrange to carry out these moves when rolling stock is available.

       Train arrangements will be made by D.A.D.R.T. Alexandria.

       Tents and camp equipment will be taken from Alexandria.

       Rations and forage for the day of entrainment and the following day will be taken from Alexandria, preserved meat and biscuit being drawn in lieu of fresh meat and bread.

       Please inform General Headquarters M.E.F. 9th Corps; and this Office as soon as arrangements for the move have been completed.

       Sd.   J.N.Broadbent.
Cairo.   Bt. Lieut. Colonel.

24th February 1916.   A.Q.M.G. The Forces In Egypt.

Copies to D.Q.M.G. M.E.F.
         D.A.G.3rd Echelon.
         C.P. M.E.F.
         D.R.T.
         D.A.D.R.T. Alex and Ismailia
         G.O.C. 9th Corps.
         D.of S, Levant Base.
         H of B Force in Egypt.

29th Division.

       For information.

26/2/16.   Lieut. Colonel.
                            A.Q.M.G. 9th Corps.

Secret

Copy No. 20

29th DIVISIONAL ORDER NO. 21

SUEZ,
27th Feby. 1916.

1. Instructions have been received that the Division is to hold itself in readiness to proceed to France at short notice.
   The attached copy of instructions for the embarkation of the Division are forwarded for information and necessary action.

2. With reference to para. 1 (1) (b) Field Ambulances and Brigade Headquarters will report as soon as possible any deficiencies in Horse Transport personnel to the O.C. Divisional Train, who will make them up to establishment.

3. With reference to para. 5 (a) Infantry Brigades will report early to these headquarters the name of the Staff Officer and Senior Officers selected, and the 29th Divisional R.A. will report the name of the Staff Officer R.A. selected.

4. With reference to para. 5 (c) Infantry Brigades, the C.R.A. and the C.R.E. will report early the names of the Officers selected to command the first line transport personnel, and the total numbers of the first line personnel and their present stations. O.C. Divisional Signals and O.C. Divisional Cyclists will also report the numbers and location of their first line transport personnel. The first line transport personnel of Divisional Headquarters, Brigade Headquarters and Field Ambulances will not proceed with the Advance parties.

5. With reference to paras. 9, 10 and 11, the C.R.A. will arrange the necessary transfers direct with the 42nd Division. There are 65 ammunition wagons available for the 29th Division at the Base. Cancelled subsequently.

6. With reference to para. 12, the transport animals allotted to Infantry Brigades, R.E., the 29th Divisional Train, and other units are placed at the disposal of the C.R.A. in order to complete the artillery teams up to establishment. The C.R.A. will arrange to draw such animals as he requires direct from Brigades or units, and will report his deficiencies direct to the A.D.R., G.H.Q.

7. Further instructions will be issued regarding the transfer of the remaining vehicles, horses and harness to the 42nd Division.

8. All helmets will be handed in to the Ordnance Depot, Port Tewfik, just prior to the departure of the troops.

9. All maps of the Canal will be collected, and handed in to these Headquarters before the departure of the troops.

10. Marching-out States of all units will be rendered by 1630 to-morrow to these Headquarters. Amendments to these States will be rendered daily by 1630 on succeeding days.

11. Receipt of this order is to be acknowledged by telegram.

C.S. Fuller
Lieut.Col. G.S.
29th Division.

Issued at 1300

INSTRUCTION RE EMBARKATION 29th DIVISION.

Headquarters,
9th CORPS.

1. The personnel of all units will proceed to France with the following modifications:-

(1) Divisional Train

(a) The supply personnel only will accompany the Division (vide para. 5 (d))

(b) A.S.C. Horse Transport personnel attached to Field Ambulances, Divisional and Brigade Head Quarters will accompany the units to which they are attached.

(2) Ambulances, Workshops will not proceed.

2. Animals and Vehicles.

No Vehicles horses or harness will accompany the Division except as under:-

(1) Officers Chargers.

(2) Gun carriages with limbers and ammunition, with teams complete.

Ammunition wagons with limbers and ammunition with teams complete.

Telephone wagons with R.A. units with teams complete.

3. Stores.

Although Vehicles do not generally speaking accompany the Division all stores except those which form part of vehicles equipment will be taken by units. Pontoons and trestles will not be taken.

4. Ammunition.

Including that carried in limbers, R.A. will take 500 rounds per gun 18.pdr.
200 " " Howr. 4.5.

5. The following are to proceed in advance of the

* 2 *

Division:-

(a) Advance parties:-

 1 Staff Officer Q.M.G. Branch.
 Senior Supply Officer.
 D. A. D. O. S.
 1 Staff Officer per Infantry Brigade.
 1 Senior Officer per Infantry Brigade.
 1 Staff Officer R.A.

(b) Personnel Divisional Squadron with Officers Chargers (Chargers if possible)

(c) Personnel of first line Transport of all formations, except as indicated in para. 1 (b) (Vide War Establishment Part VII, as to what is the official composition of first line Trabsport) The first line Transport personnel should be in command of an officer as follows:-

 Each Infantry Brigade   1 Officer.
 R.A. Division   1 Officer
 R.E. of Division and any other units.   1 Officer.

(d) Supply personnel of Divisional Train vide para 1 (a)

6. The following units will accompany the Division:-

 5 Depot Units of Supply.) To be detailed
 1 Field Bakery.   ) by I.G.C.
 1 Field Butchery.   )
 29th Divisional Base Depot.
 29th Division Record Section, 3rd Echelon.
 All Base kits.

7. All details enumerated in para. 5 must be ready at short notice to start on receipt of telegraphic orders.

8. The Division other than those in para. 5 will probably be required to commence embarkation about 6th March.

9. All 18-pdr. guns and carriages at present with the 29th Division are to be exchanged at once with those with the 42nd Division. They should be stripped prior to exchange.

* 3 *

10. The Wheels with Sand Tyres are to remain with the 42nd Division, the 29th Division retaining wheels without Sand tyres.

11. The 29th Division are to make up any deficiencies in Wagons Ammunition with Limbers by drawing on the 42nd Division. Any such Wagons with Sand Tyres are to have them removed before transfer.

12. To enable the vehicles enumerated in para. 2 (2) to be completed in animals, all suitable animals in the 29th Division should be transferred to the Artillery at once; any shortage in animals to be reported as soon as possible to A.D.R.,G.H.Q., by telegram.

13. All vehicles, horses and harness not accompanying the 29th Division will be transferred to 42nd Division under Corps instructions.

(Sgd) Walter Campbell

G.H.Q.,
26/2/16.

Major General,
D.Q.M.G.,M.E.F.

Copies to 42nd Div.
G.S.
"A"
I.G.C. Levbase.

"A" Form.
MESSAGES AND SIGNALS.
Army Form C. 2121.

TO
86 Brigade
87
88

Sender's Number: GA 216.
Day of Month: 7/2
AAA

Reference para 5 G.S Memo No 39 and para 10 of 29th Div Order No 21 the machine gun companies are from this date to be considered as a separate unit attached to Brigades aaa They will therefore render separate marching out states. aaa Reference instructions re Embarkation 29th Division para 5(C) and 29th Div Order No 21 para 4 all battalion transport officers will proceed with the advanced parties, the senior transport officer in each Brigade to take command of the transport personnel.

D. M. Copp

From: 29th Div
Place:
Time: 1750.

"A" Form.
MESSAGES AND SIGNALS.

Army Form C. 2121.

TO: 3= Echelon ALEXANDRIA

Sender's Number.	Day of Month	In reply to Number	
G.539.	27°		AAA

Instructions have been received that the 29° Division Record Section is to hold itself in readiness to embark at an early date. Further information will be sent later. Pse acknowledge

From 29 Dsn
Time 1537

"A" Form. Army Form C. 2121.

MESSAGES AND SIGNALS.   No. of Message_____

Prefix____ Code____ m.	Words	Charge	This message is on a/c of:	Recd. at____ m.
Office of Origin and Service Instructions.	Sent		____Service.	Date ⑦
____	At____ m.			From____
____	To____			
____	By____		(Signature of "Franking Officer.")	By____

TO { 29th Division Base Depot ALEXANDRIA.

Sender's Number.	Day of Month	In reply to Number	AAA
G.537	27th		

Instructions have been received that you are to hold yourself in readiness to embark with all base kits at an early date. Further information will be sent later. Acknowledge.

From: 29th Divn
Place:
Time: 1535

G.F. Fuller
ADA

The above may be forwarded as now corrected.   (Z)
_____   _____
Censor.   Signature of Addressor or person authorised to telegraph in his name.

* This line should be erased if not required.

(688-9) —McC. & Co., Ltd., London.— W 14142/641. 225,000. 4/15. Forms C 2121/10.

"C" Form (Quadruplicate).   Army Form C 2123 A

MESSAGES AND SIGNALS.

No. of Message..........

Charges to Pay   Office Stamp.
£   s.   d.

Service Instructions   Cairo Bg

Handed in at the .... Office, at 2380 m. Received here at 0215 m.

TO   Hdqrs 29th Divn
      Suez

Sender's Number.	Day of Month.	In reply to Number.	
			AAA
			G.537
No	1119	your	754
of	date	received	

FROM   Commanding Base Depot
PLACE
TIME

Wt. 1753.—A. W. & Co.—40,000 Pads. 6/15.

"A" Form.   Army Form C. 2121.
MESSAGES AND SIGNALS.   No. of Message_____

Prefix____ Code____ m. | Words | Charge |
Office of Orig. nd Service Instructions.   This message is on a/c of: Recd. at_____ m.
                          Sent   Date (8)
                       At_____ m.   _____Service.   From
                       To   By
                       By_____ (Signature of "Franking Officer.")

TO { 29/Division

Sender's Number | Day of Month | In reply to Number | AAA
QH 742 | 29/2 | |

Para 5 b CMQ 445 db 26/2
refers to "squadron charges
only aaa Orders re
rations will be issued
by Communications aaa
SAA to be taken per man
220 per gun 16500 to
be taken from SUEZ.
aaa ad

From 9/Corps
Place
Time 1905
                The above may be forwarded as now corrected. (Z) Wheatham
                                                   Censor.   Signature of Addressee or person authorised to telegraph in his name.
                * This line should be erased if not required.

"A" Form.
MESSAGES AND SIGNALS.
Army Form C. 2121.

Prefix	Code	m.	Words	Charge	This message is on a/c of:	No. of Message
Office of Origin and Service Instructions.			Sent At ... m. To By		...... Service. (Signature of "Franking Officer.")	Recd. at ...... m. Date From By

TO 86th, 87th & 88th Bdes
DaDOS

Sender's Number.	Day of Month	In reply to Number	
G 569	29th		A A A

Refer Instructions for embarkation from G.H.Q para 5(b) Officers Chargers from Bde will not accompany advance party AAA S.A.A to be taken 220 per man and 16500 per machine gun AAA Addressed all Bdes & DaDOS.

From 29th Divn
Place
Time 2150.

The above may be forwarded as now corrected.   (Z)

C O P Y.

GENERAL HEADQUARTERS,
MEDITERRANEAN EXPEDITIONARY FORCE.
26th February 1916.

I.G.C.
C/o Levbase.

As far as possible the 29th Division, except advance parties, should embark in the following order in flights of :-

One Infantry Brigade.
One F.A. Brigade.
One Company R.E.
One Field Ambulance.

2. Divisional Headquarters and Divisional Signal Company should follow the first flight.

3. Add one Howitzer Brigade to the 2nd Flight.

4. The Third Flight will be followed by the Newfoundland Regiment and other Divisional Units not enumerated above.

5. There is no Divisional Ammunition Column belonging to the 29th Division, but the one Officer and 35 Other Ranks detailed for care of ammunition should proceed with the last Flight.

6. All details as regards the embarkation are to be arranged direct with 9th Corps.

7. Programmes should be forwarded to G.H.Q. for Information and Progress Reports rendered.

8. 9th Corps will render as soon as possible to I.G.C. Savoy Hotel, Cairo, Marching out states for all Units and keep him informed of any material changes.

(Signed)   Walter Campbell.

Major General.
D.Q.M.G., M.E.F.

Headquarters,
9th Corps.

With reference to G.H.Q. letter of the 26th inst., addressed to the I.G.C., c/o Lovebase, the following is the proposed arrangement of flights for embarkation :-

<u>1st Flight.</u>

    87th Infantry Brigade,

    17th F.A. Brigade,

    1/1st West Riding Field Co.,

    87th Field Ambulance,

29th Divisional Headquarters, Divisional R.A. and R.E. Headquarters; 29th Divisional Signal Co.; 29th Divisional Cyclists, and Divisional Band.

<u>2nd Flight.</u>

    86th Infantry Brigade,

    15th H.A. Brigade

    57th Howitzer F.A. Brigade

    1/3rd Kent Field Co. R.E.

    89th Field Ambulance.

<u>3rd Flight.</u>

    88th Infantry Brigade (including Newfoundland Battalion),

    147th F.A. Brigade,

    1/2nd London Field Co., R.E.,

    88th Field Ambulance,

    Divisional Ammunition Section,

    18th Mobile Veterinary Section.

9th Corps   2.

    2. Marching Out States of the Units of the Division are attached.   Details regarding weights of Baggage will be forwarded later.

17CM

                                  Brigadier General,

28/2/16.   Commanding 29th Division.

"A" Form.
Army Form C. 2121.
MESSAGES AND SIGNALS.

TO   29/ Division

Sender's Number.	Day of Month	In reply to Number	
*Q.N.649	26/2	G.A.201	A A A

G.H.Q. informs me that Brigades will be completed to four batteries on arrival in France.

From 4/Corps
Place
Time 0945

Copy No. 6

10th (INDIAN) DIVISION OPERATION ORDER No.17.

29th February 1916.

On the withdrawal of units of the 29th Division to the West Bank of the Canal, moves will take place as follows :-

1st March 1916.

```
15th Brigade R.H.A.    EL SHATT to SUEZ CAMP.
17th    "    R.F.A.    AYUN MUSSA to SUEZ CAMP.
2 Bns. 87th Brigade    EL KUBRI E. to SUEZ CAMP.
Headquarters 29th Brigade )  EL SHATT to EL KUBRI E.
57th Rifles               )
1 Company 86th Brigade  GURKHA POST to EL KUBRI E.
(On relief by 1 Company 42nd Division.
58th Rifles      )  AYUN MUSSA to EL SHATT.
Alwar Infantry   )
```

2nd March 1916.

```
Headquarters & 2 Bns. 86th Brigade EL KUBRI to SUEZ CAMP.
57th Rifles  EL KUBRI E. to RAILHEAD with 1 Company to
                                              HALFWAY HOUSE.
1 Company Royal Fusiliers  HALFWAY HOUSE to EL KUBRI E.
23rd Pioneers  RAILHEAD EL SHATT to DARB EL HAJ and CREWE
                                                       POST.
Dublin Fusiliers  DARB EL HAJ & CREWE POST to EL KUBRI E.
Alwar Infantry  EL SHATT to RAILHEAD EL SHATT.
Patiala Infantry  EL SHATT to EL KUBRI E.
```

3rd March 1916.

Two Bns. 86th Brigade to SUEZ CAMP.

Details of timings for the crossing of EL KUBRI Bridge on 1st March, and for transport are on Table "A" attached to this order.

Reports to be made to 10th (Indian) Division as soon as each move is completed.

W.F. Bainbridge

~~Captain,~~
~~for~~ Lieut: Colonel,
Issued at 15.40.   General Staff, 10th (Indian) Division.

```
Copy Nos.1 and 2 Office.
  "   No. 3 War Diary.
  "   Nos.4 and 5 9th Corps.
  "   No. 6 29th Division.
  "    "   7 A.Q.M.G.
  "    "   8 A.D.M.S.
  "    "   9 A.D.S.&.T.
  "    "  10 20th Brigade.
  "    "  11 29th Brigade.
  "    "  12 86th Brigade.
  "    "  13 C.R.E.
  "    "  14 C.R.A., 29th Division.
```

Unit.	Location.	Destination.	Nature of transport etc.	Time of crossing El Kubri Bridge.	Date of move.
2 Bns. 87th Brigade.	El Kubri E.	Suez Camp.	Provided by 29th Divn.	6.30 a.m.	1-3-16.
15th Brigade R.H.A.	El Shatt.	"	—do—	7.30 a.m.	=do=
17th Brigade R.F.A.	Ayun Mussa.	"	—do—	8.0 a.m.	=do=
Hd.Qrs. 29th Brigade.	El Shatt.	El Kubri E.	Water.	---	-do-
57th Rifles.	"	"	"	---	-do-
Alwar Infantry.	Ayun Mussa.	El Shatt.)	1st Line transport of units 20th Bde. and camel transport.	---	-do-
58th Rifles.	"	" ")			
1 Company 86th Brigade.	No.4 Post.	El Kubri E.	Camels from El Kubri E.	---	-do-
Hd.Qrs.& 2 Bns.86th Brigade.	El Kubri E.	Suez Camp.	From 29th Division.	7.0 a.m.	2-3-16.
57th Rifles less 1 Company.	" "	Railhead El Kubri.	Rail.	---	=do=
1 Company 57th Rifles.	Halfway House.	Halfway House.	Camel from Kubri.	---	=do=
1 Royal Fusiliers.	Railhead El Shatt.	El Kubri E.	" " El Shatt.	---	=do=
23rd Pioneers.	El Shatt.	Darb el Haj & Crewe Post.	" "	---	=do=
Alwar Infantry.	Darb el Haj and Crewe Post.	Railhead El Shatt.	Rail.	---	-do-
Dublin Fusiliers.	" "	El Kubri E.	Camel and Rail.	---	-do-
Patiala Infantry.	El Shatt.	El Kubri E.	Water.	---	-do-
Dublin Fusiliers.	El Kubri E.	Suez Camp.	From 29th Division.	7.0 a.m.	3-3-16.
Royal Fusiliers.	" "	" "	=do=	8.0 a.m.	-do-

GENERAL HEADQUARTERS,
MEDITERRANEAN EXPEDITIONARY FORCE.

29th February 1916.

Headquarters,
9th CORPS,
SUEZ.

Reference my C.M.Q.445 of 26th, paragraph 5.(Q) should be cancelled and now read as follows:-

(a) Advance parties:-

   (1) For disembarkation and entrainment:-

      1 Officer Divisional Staff.
      3 Officers from Division for entraining duties.
      6 Subalterns as A.M.L.O's.

   (2) For detrainment and billeting duties:-

      1 Staff Officer from "Q" Branch Divisional Staff.
      1 Staff Officer from each Infantry Brigade
      1 Staff Officer Divisional Artillery.
      Senior Supply Officer of Division.
      Divisional Ordnance Officer.
      Deputy Assistant Director Medical Services of the Division.

(Sgd) E.R. O'Hara
for Lt. Colonel,
A.Q.M.G., M.E.F.

Copies to:- 29th Division.
G.S.
A.
I.G.C., LEVBASE.

Headquarters,
29th Division,
SUEZ CAMP.

For information.

Lt. Colonel,
A.Q.M.G., M.E.F.

Appx I

(1 - 12)

SECRET.

Appendix I

~~Headquarters,~~

~~9th Corps.~~

The following officers will proceed to Port Said Wednesday evening March 1st. to embark on "Llandovery Castle". For disembarkation and entrainment, one Divisional Staff Officer. Three officers from Division for entraining duties, six subalterns as Assistant M.L.O's. For detrainment and billetting duties, one Staff Officer from "Q" Branch Divisional Staff, one Staff Officer from each Infantry Brigade, one Staff Officer Divisional Artillery, Senior Supply Officer of Division, D.A.D.O.S., and D.A.D.M.S.

Divisional Staff Officer — Lt.Col.L.H.Abbott (at Marseilles)

Staff Officer Q.M.G.Branch — Capt.L.C.Morgan.

Senior Supply Officer — Capt.J.G.Gillam.

D.A.D.O.S. — Capt.J.H.Grieve.

D.A.D.M.S. — Capt.H.F.Panton.

Staff Officers.

86th Brigade. — Capt. Gee, 2nd Royal Fusiliers.

87th Brigade. — Capt.C.S.Stirling Cookson,1/K.O.S.B.

88th Brigade. — Capt.Kearns, 4th Worcesters.

R.A. — Lieut. Drummond Hay.

Three Officers Entraining Duties.

2/Lieut. Creaney, 2nd S.Wales Borderers.

Capt. Moffat, 1st R.Dublin Fusiliers.

2/Lieut. ~~Stewart~~ Graham, 1/5th Royal Scots.

A.M.L.O's

Capt. A.E. Stokes-Roberts, 4th Worcester Regt.

2/Lieut. Mackie, 1/5th Royal Scots.

2.

2.

    Lieut.V.Gordon,   1st K.O.S.B.

    Lieut.Paterson,   1st K.O.S.B.

    2/Lieut. Mac.D.Campbell, 1st Lancashire Fusiliers.

    2/Lieut. Simpson,   1st R.Munster Fusiliers.

                                                        Brigadier General,

1st March 1916.   Commanding 29th Division.

C.R. 15584/Q/1.

The

 General Officer Commanding

  9th. Army Corps,

   S U E Z.

----

1. The Surrey Yeomanry Squadron - Divisional Cavalry to the 29th. Division - will embark in the H.T. "NESSIAN", at ALEXANDRIA, for MARSEILLES on the 3rd. March, 1916.

2. No horses except Officers' chargers and no vehicles will be taken.

3. The ship will be rationed at Alexandria with ten days' voyage rations and forage.

4. Tents will not be taken.

5. Tea will be the first meal issued on board ship on the day of embarkation. Units embarking should therefore have with them the unexpired portion of the day's rations.

6. Four copies of special embarkation return and four copies of nominal rolls of those embarking will be required by the Embarkation Staff Officer.

              [signature]

                Bt. Lt. Colonel,

Cairo,   For
1st. March, 1916.   Inspector General of
              Communications.

Copies to ---
  D.Q.M.G. G.H.Q.   N.T.O. ALEX.
  D.A.G. 3rd. Ech.   G.O.C. 29th. Division.
  C.P. M.E.F.   Base Commdt., ALEX.
  G.O.C., ALEX. (FOR ACTION) D. of S. L.B.
  E.S.O., ALEX.   H. of B. F.E.
  P.N.T.O. EGYPT.

                   d

"A" Form.				Army Form C. 2121.
MESSAGES AND SIGNALS.				No. of Message

Prefix	Code	m.	Words	Charge	This message is on a/c of:	Recd. at	③	m.
Office of Origin and Service Instructions.			Sent		Service.	Date		
			At	m.		From		
			To			By		
			By		(Signature of "Franking Officer.")			

TO	C.R.E. and D.A.D.O.S.

Sender's Number.	Day of Month	In reply to Number	
G.576	1		AAA

Mounted RE will take 50 rounds and dismounted RE 100 rounds S.A.A. per man on embarkation addressed CRE repeated DADOS.

From	29 Div
Place	
Time	1555

"C" Form (Quadruplicate).   Army Form C 2123/A

MESSAGES AND SIGNALS.

No. of Message...... 4

| Charges to Pay | Office Stamp |
| £   s.   d. | |

Service Instructions: Priority GHQ

Handed in at the .... Office, at 1422 m. Received here at 1454 m.

TO: 29th Division

Sender's Number	Day of Month	In reply to Number	AAA
CMQ 1835	1st		

XHYTP	OPIZM	GHBSB	KIATZ
RCZNO	VZIIL	TQSKN	KIKSC
XZPYI	VFVEP	FLQIM	FVZEU
ERBQH	EETLY	TCNSZ	TPSET
YCBEP	YETBA	RXLIA	XVLKN
IPSPN	YHPAY	IACZQ	

Addressed 29th Division
Repeated 9th Corps and
Daglock

The Cable section personnel will go with 29th Div, all stores to be taken other than actual vehicle equipment.

D.O.

FROM / PLACE / TIME: GHQ Medforce

Wt. 1753.—A. W. & Co.—40,000 Pads. 6/15.

"A" Form.
MESSAGES AND SIGNALS.
Army Form C. 2121.

TO 9th Corps

Sender's Number: GA 232
Day of Month: 1/3

Reference CM&T 835 cipher message - Understand you are making all arrangements for embarkation of Cable Section aaa we are not therefore including the personnel etc in our returns.

D. Myler
JS

From: 29th Div
Time: 1553

"C" Form (Quadruplicate).   Army Form C 2123 A

MESSAGES AND SIGNALS.

No. of Message...............

31

Charges to Pay £ s. d.

Office Stamp.

Service Instructions

Handed in at the .... Office, at ... 1902 ...m. Received here at ... 19 ...

TO   29th Divn

Sender's Number.	Day of Month.	In reply to Number.	
N 453	1/3	Ga 232	AAA

Your should take necessary
action with regards to
G.G. cable section aaa
O.C. 9th Corps signal
Co will give all
particulars required

FROM PLACE TIME   9th Corps   1900

"B" Form.
MESSAGES AND SIGNALS.

Army Form C. 2122.

Prefix BJS Code FL		Received	Sent	No. of Message
Office of Origin and Service Instructions.	Words.	At 1904 m.	At m.	Office Stamp.
Priority ICO	63	From ICO By Olive	To By	

TO { 29/ Divn

Sender's Number	Day of Month	In reply to Number	
QN 798	March 3		AAA

Reference our conversation on telephone tonight and 453/16 dated 29 Feb when instructing FERIAL re 57th How Bde will you arrange for advance party transport personnel of that bde numbering 1 officer and 35 other ranks to proceed to PORT SAID aaa These were not shown in above letter aaa Addressed Daglock repeated 29th Divn

From **Ninth Corps**
Place
Time **1836**

* This line should be erased if not required.

"A" Form.
MESSAGES AND SIGNALS.
Army Form C. 2121.

Prefix	Code	m.	Words	Charge	This message is on a/c of:	Recd. at	m.

Office of Origin and Service Instructions:
Priority

Sent At ___ m.
To ___
By ___

___Service.
(Signature of "Franking Officer.")

Date ___
From ___
By ___

TO: 9th Corps

Sender's Number	Day of Month	In reply to Number	
G.604	3.	Q.N.790	AAA

Advance party 1st line transport personnel for 57th Howr Bde are not included in numbers forwarded with my A/461/4 of 29th ult AAA They amount to 1 Offr and 35 other Rks approx. AAA Will you obtain instructions from G.H.Q. whether they are to sail so that they may be warned.

From: 29th Divn
Place:
Time: 1645.

C. Lall.
Lt Col. G.S.

"C" Form (Quadruplicate). Army Form C 2123 A
MESSAGES AND SIGNALS.   No. of Message...

25   Charges to Pay Office Stamp

Service Instructions

Handed in at the ......C.P...... Office, at ....16.00... m. Received here at ......

TO   29th Divn

Sender's Number.	Day of Month.	In reply to Number.	AAA
1530	2		

Marching out state 460th
Howitzer battery RFA officers
6 other ranks 158
animals 44 guns 4
vehicles 14

FROM   29th Da
PLACE
TIME

Wt. 1753.—A. W. & Co.—40,000 Pads. 6/15.

(4005) Wt. W 1789-1402. 5 15. 48,000 Pads. S. B. Ltd.

"B" Form.

Army Form C 2122

MESSAGES AND SIGNALS.

No. of Message _____

⑦

Prefix	Code ____ m.	Received	Sent	Office Stamp.
Office of Origin and Service Instructions. CP	Words. 32	At 1245 m. From CP By mal	At ____ m. To ____ By ____	YB 3-4-16

TO {	29th Devon		
* Sender's Number SC 1230	Day of Month 3	In reply to Number	AAA

Please	note	the	following	will
also	proceed	in	advance	aaa
1	officer	1	Sgt	21
other	ranks	1st	Line	transport
personnel	of	m.	gun	coy

From: 87th Bde
Place:
Time:

* This line should be erased if not required

"A" Form.
Army Form C. 2121.

MESSAGES AND SIGNALS.

Prefix	Code	m.	Words	Charge	This message is on a/c of:	Recd. at	m.
Office of Origin and Service Instructions.			Sent		............Service.	Date (8)	
			At m.			From	
			To			By	
			By		(Signature of "Franking Officer.")		

TO — 9th Corps

Sender's Number.	Day of Month	In reply to Number	
G 595	2nd		A A A

Ref my A/461/4 of 29th ult departure of 460th Battery returns artillery advance party as 3 offrs 198 other Ranks.

From: 29 Divn
Place:
Time: 1845

(Z)

Censor.   Signature of Addressor or person authorised to telegraph in his name.

* This line should be erased if not required.
(774-5)—McC. & Co. Ltd., London.—W 1789/1402. 150,000. 8/15. Forms C 2121/10.

Secret

Copy No 4532 29/2/16

Headquarters,
9th Army Corps.

Reference your C.M.Q. 445, dated 26/2/16 Para. 5, (a),(c),(d), attached is list of Officers and other Ranks, who will proceed with Advance Party.

Those marked with an asterisk have been warned to be ready to embark on March 2nd vide your telegram Q.N.731. The DADMS, the 3 Div. Officers for embarkation duties & the 6 Subaltern officers for AMLO's have also been warned for 2nd March

Sgd. C.G. Fuller, Lt Col G.S.
for. Brigadier General,
Commanding 29th Division.

29th February 1916.

Officers marked ✓ have departed - 2-3-16.

Staff Officer Q.M.G.Branch. ✓   Capt. M.C.Morgan. *
Senior Supply Officer. ✓   Capt. J.G.Gillam.
D.A.D.O.S. ✓   Capt. J.H.Grieve. *
Supply Section Train. ✓   8 Officers and 57 Other
                                                        Ranks.
D.A.D.M.S   ✓   Capt. H.F. Panton *

ADVANCE PARTY.

86th Brigade.   Senior Officer. ✓   Capt. Pottle, 2nd Royal Fus. Lancs

                 Staff Officer. ✓   Capt. Gee, 2nd Royal Fus. *
                                           G

                 Transport Officer. Lieut. Newenham, 1st R.Munster
                                                      Fusiliers.
                                                1 Offr sailed ✓
                 Transport Personnel. 3 Officers and 156 Other
                                                  Ranks at ~~Knoickfest~~.

87th Brigade.   Senior Officer. ✓   Major Meiklejohn, 1st Border
                                                              Regt.

                 Staff Officer. ✓   Capt. C.S.Stirling Cookson, *
                                              1st K.O.S.B.

                 Transport Officer. ✓ Lieut. Long, 1st K.O.S.B.

S.W.B. 1 Offr – 31 O.Rks
K.O.S.B 1 "   31 "   } Transport Personnel. 3 Officers and 124
R.I.F. 1 "   31 "   Other Ranks.
Border 1 "   31 "

88th Brigade.   Senior Officer. ✓   Major A.V.Clutterbuck, 1/Essex.

                 Staff Officer. ✓   Capt. Kearns, 4th Worcesters *

H.Q — 1 5 Other Rks   Transport Officer. 2/Lieut. J.A.Smithin, 4th
Essex   1 Offr 32   Worcesters.
Hants   1 "   32   2 Offrs sailed ✓
Worsters 1 "   33   }   Transport Personnel. 4 Officers and 167 Other
R.Scots 1 "   33   Ranks.
N.F.L.D 1 —   32

29th Div. Artillery.   RESERVE, 3   198
                 Transport Personnel.   4 Officers and ~~255~~ Other
                                                         Ranks.
3 Bdes at 62 = 186   2/Lt G.H.Barker – 15th Bde (in command)
                      2/Lt H.R. Remington – 17th Bde. 2/Lt E.L. Kidd – 147th Bde.
Spare Personnel 3 Offrs & 74 12   Staff Officer RA. Lieut Drummond Hay *
     4 Offrs & 235 Other Ranks
     3   198

Royal Engineers. Transport Officer. Lieut. J.K.B.Langley,
                                           1st W.Riding Fd.Coy.R.E.

                 Transport Personnel.   95 Other Ranks.

Vide wire   { Divl. Signals   1 Officer and 39 other Rks
G.574.   { Divl. Cyclists   2 other Ranks.

A.A. & Q.M.G.,
    29th Division.

      Will you kindly issue instructions that Units before leaving Camp will strike their Tents, and return them to the A/D.A.D.O.S., 29th Division. Units should also return all surplus Ordnance Stores as early as possible to the same place.

                                    R.S. Hamilton
                                         Lt.Colonel,

1/3/16.   A.D.O.S., 9th Corps.

"O" Form (Triplicate).   Army Form C 2123 A
MESSAGES AND SIGNALS.   No. of Message... 11

DDW   49   Copy   Charges to Pay   Office Stamp
        Mac

Service Instructions

Handed in at the ...HCO... Office, at ...1623... m. Received here at ...1704... m.

TO: 29th Division

Sender's Number	Day of Month	In reply to Number	
In/62	1st March		AAA
All	surplus	vehicles	and
and	animals	from	29th Div
will	be	handed	in
to	29th	Div.	Train
Suez	Camp	aaa	42nd
Div	requirements	will	be
filled	from	that	unit
and	balance	of	vehicles
handed	over	to	ordnance
Suez	Camp	aaa	Acknowledge
			10 pm on Friday night

FROM: Ninth Corps
PLACE:
TIME: 1610.

"A" Form. Army Form C. 2121.
MESSAGES AND SIGNALS.   No. of Message_____

Prefix_____Code_____m.	Words	Charge	This message is on a/c of :	Recd. at_____m.
Office of Origin and Service Instructions.				Date_____
_____	Sent		_____Service.	From_____
_____	At_____m.			
_____	To_____			
_____	By_____		(Signature of "Franking Officer.")	By_____

TO { CRA 88th Bde
86 Bde 29th Div Train
87 D.A.Q.M.G.

| Sender's Number | Day of Month | In reply to Number | **AAA** |
| GA 231 | 1/3 | | |

The CRA will arrange to select all animals required from 1st line transport 87th and 88th Brigades this afternoon and will take them over tomorrow morning units returning the remainder together with all vehicles to the Div: Train aaa On receipt of these animals the O.C Train will hand over to the Artillery Train such animals as are required by the Artillery by them aaa The 86th Brigade will hand over all animals of their 1st line transport as are required by the Artillery on the evening of the 3rd inst. any animals remaining to be handed over to the Div Train on the same date together with all vehicles aaa addressed CRA all Brigades repeated 29th Div Train repeated D.A.Q.M.G.

From 29th Div
Place
Time

The above may be forwarded as now corrected.   (Z)

Censor. Signature of Addresser or person authorised to telegraph in his name.

* This line should be erased if not required.

"A" Form.
MESSAGES AND SIGNALS.
Army Form C. 2121.

Prefix	Code	m.	Words	Charge	This message is on a/c of:	Recd. at	m.
Office of Origin and Service Instructions.			Sent			Date	
			At	m.	Service.	From	
			To			By	
			By		(Signature of "Franking Officer.")		

TO — 9th Corps.

Sender's Number.	Day of Month	In reply to Number	
G.593	2	Q.N.76?	AAA

Recd ~~ammunition tonight~~

From 29. Div.
Place
Time 1032

The above may be forwarded as now corrected.   (Z)

FOR OFFICERS USE ONLY.

The following officers *with 17 servants* proceeded to Port Said on March 1st 1916. to embark on "Landovery Castle":-

Divisional Staff Officer	- Lt.Col.L.H.Abbott, (at Marseilles)
Staff Officer, Q.M.S.Branch.	- Capt.M.C.Morgan.
Senior Supply Officer.	- Capt.J.G.Gillam.
D.A.D.O.S.	- Capt.J.H.Greive.
D.A.D.M.S.	- Capt.H.F.Panton.
Staff Officer, R.F.A.	- Lieut.Drummond Hay.

Staff Officers.

86th Infantry Brigade.	- Capt.Gee, 2/Royal Fus.
87th Infantry Brigade.	- Capt.C.S.Stirling Cookson 1/K.O.S.B,
88th Infantry Brigade.	- Capt.Kearns, 4th Worcs.

Three Officers Entraining Duties.

2/Lt. Creany,	- 2nd S.Wales Borderers.
Capt. Moffat,	- 1st R.Dublin Fusiliers.
Lieut. Stewart,	- 1/5th Royal Scots.

A.M.L.O's.

Capt.Stokes-Roberts.	- 4th Worcester Regt.
2/Lieut.Mackie.	- 1/5th Royal Scots.
Lieut.V.Gordon,	- 1st K.O.S.B's.
Lieut. Paterson,	- 1st K.O.S.B's.
2/Lt. Mac.D.Campbell	- 1st Lancs. Fusiliers.
2/Lt. Simpson,	- 1st R.Munster Fusiliers.

Appx 2

(1 — 2)

SECRET.

Appendix 2

Headquarters,
    9th Corps.

With reference to G.H.Q. telegram No. 4405, of 1st instant, the following details will leave Suez to-morrow evening by the 1730 train for Alexandria, to make up the balance of 15 Officers and 64 Other Ranks required to complete the "CESTRIAN" and "NESSIAN".

86th BRIGADE.

    Senior Officer   Capt. Pottle, 2nd Royal Fus.

    One transport Officer
        and two servants.

87th BRIGADE.

    Senior Officer   Major Meiklejohn, 1st Border Regt.

    One transport Officer
        and two servants.

88th BRIGADE.

    Senior Officer   Major Clutterbuck, 1st Essex Regt.

    Two transport Officers
        and three servants.

Supply Section of Train.   8 Officers and 57 Other Ranks.

    Total: 15 Officers and 64 Other Ranks.

Brigadier General.
Commanding 29th Division.

1st March 1916.

Following details totalling 15 officers and 64 other ranks will entrain on 2nd instant at SUEZ RUE COLMAR Station by 1730 train for ALEXANDRIA for embarkation on NESSIAN and CESTRIAN.

86th Brigade.

  Captain Pottle. 2nd Royal Fus.   Senior Officer.
* 2/Lt.Donnes. 1st Lancs.Fus.   Transport Officer.
  and 2 servants.

87th Brigade.

  Major Meiklejohn. 1st Border Regt.   Senior Officer.
  Lieut.Long. 1st K.O.S.B.   Transport Officer.
  and 2 servants.

88th Brigade.

  Major Clutterbuck. 1st Essex Regt.   Senior Officer.
  Lt.H.C.Herden. Newfoundland Regt.   Transport Officer.
  2/Lt.T.Newlands. 1/5th Royal Scots. Transport Officer.
  and 3 servants.

Supply Section of Train.

  8 Officers and 57 other ranks.

* 2/Lt.Donnes will entrain at KUBRI.

            Lieut.Colonel, G.S.
2nd March 1916.   29th Division.

Diverted to Port Said, on arrival at Alexandria, to embark on "MANITOU".

3/3/16

Div: Squadron 7 Offrs 136 O.Rks. embarked on the "NESSIAN." m 3/21

Received at 1518.

To G.O.C. 9th Corps (Cipher).

No. 4405   1/3/15.

Reference embarkation of advance parties of 29th Division for MARSEILLES there will be room for 22 Officers and 200 men on the CESTRIAN and NESSIAN embarking at Alexandria on 3rd March AAA Propose to embark Surrey Yeomanry strength 7 Officers 136 Other Ranks and officers chargers on the NESSIAN AAA Will you send details from SUEZ to make up numbers AAA They should reach ALEXANDRIA early morning 3rd March AAA Addressed 9th Corps repeated Q.M.G., G.H.Q.

DAGLOCK.

appx. 3

(1 - 5.)

SECRET.   Copy No.21

F O R C E   O R D E R   No. 12.

by

GENERAL SIR ARCHIBALD MURRAY, K.C.B., K.C.M.G., C.V.O., D.S.O.

Commander-in-Chief, Mediterranean Expeditionary Force.

GENERAL HEADQUARTERS.

3rd. March 1916.

(1).   The following further amendments are made to Force Order No.5 of January 27th. 1916:-

    (a)   The 10th. Indian Division and 31st. Division cease to form part of the Mediterranean Expeditionary Force.

    (b)   The 20th. and 29th. Indian Infantry Brigades will be attached to the 42nd. Division.

(2)   The following further amendments are made in the distribution of artillery as detailed in Force Order No. 5 and amended in Force Order No. 8, of February 11th. :-

    (a)   The 132nd. Field Artillery (Howitzer) Brigade is allotted to the 29th. Division. The designation of the batteries of this brigade will be altered as follows:-

    460th. Battery will become 'A' Battery, 132nd. F.A.B.

    'A' Battery 57th. F.A.B. will become 'B' Battery 132nd. F.A.B.

    'D' Battery 57th. F.A.B. will become 'C' Battery 132nd. F.A.B.

    (b)   90th. Heavy Battery is transferred from 9th. Army Corps to 1st. A.& N.Z. Army Corps, and will form part of the 35th. Brigade, R.G.A., in place of the 131st. Heavy Battery.

    (c)   54th. and 55th. Siege Batteries cease to form part of 1st. A.& N.Z. Army Corps Artillery.

    (d)   'A' and 'B' Batteries, H.A.C., will be attached to 4th. and 1st. Mounted Brigades respectively.

(2)

(e) 3rd. and 4th. T.F.R.H.A. Brigades will form Divisional Artillery, A.& N.Z. Mounted Division.

(Signed) A. LYNDEN BELL.
MAJOR GENERAL.
Chief of the General Staff.
Mediterranean Expeditionary Force.

29th. Division.

For information.

Brigadier General
General Staff.
9th. Army Corps.

"A" Form.
Army Form C. 2121.

MESSAGES AND SIGNALS.

Prefix	Code	m.	Words	Charge	This message is on a/c of:	Recd. at ② m.
Office of Origin and Service Instructions.			Sent		Service.	Date
			At m.			From
			To			By
			By		(Signature of "Franking Officer.")	

TO   9ᵗʰ Corps

Sender's Number.	Day of Month	In reply to Number	AAA
* G.549.	28ᵗʰ		

Please wire 3ʳᵈ Echelon to send Captain Ferrier RA and 35 other Ranks RA to join 29ᵗʰ Div Ammun Section at SUEZ CAMP aaa also to send any other details available to make up Divisional Artillery up to establishment

C.F.

From 29ᵗʰ Divn
Place
Time 1733.

The above may be forwarded as now corrected. (Z)

Censor. Signature of Addressor or person authorised to telegraph in his name.

* This line should be erased if not required.

(4005) Wt. W.1789-1402. 5 15. 48,000 Pads. S. B. Ltd.
"B" Form.   Army Form C 2122

MESSAGES AND SIGNALS.

No. of Message _____

Prefix _____ Code _____
Office of Origin and Service Instructions: **Suez Camp**
Words: 27
Received At **1832** m.   From **CP**   By **Hayward**
Sent At ___ m.   To ___   By ___
Office Stamp.

TO { **29th Divn** }

Sender's Number: **BM/303**
Day of Month: **3rd**
In reply to Number:
AAA

Are steps being taken please
by you to make up
deficiencies in O.R. or
should I wire 3rd Echelon
direct

Wired 9: Corps on 28:
Capt Fraser + 35 others and
amp.

From **89/ DA**
Place
Time

This line should be erased if not required.

"A" Form.
Army Form C. 2121.

MESSAGES AND SIGNALS.

TO	29 Div RA

Sender's Number.	Day of Month	In reply to Number	
G606	3/10	B.M. 303	A A A

Corps were asked on 28th to send Capt Fraser and 35 other Rks to Divl Amm Sect also any other details available to make up Divl Amm to establishment.

From: 29th Divn
Place:
Time: 1922

C.R.15394/Q/1.

The
General Officer Commanding
9th. Corps, S U E Z.
----

1. The H.T. MANITOU will be ready to embark the advanced parties of the 29th. Division at Port Said on Sunday, 5th. March, 1916.

2. An Infantry train (emergancy) will be ready for loading at Suez Camp at 1 a.m. and will leave for Port Said at 2.40 a.m. arriving Port Said at 8.15 a.m. on the 5th. March, 1916.

3. All details shown in your 453.Q. of the 29th. instant, amounting to 24 officers, 879 other ranks, together with the 359th. Depot Unit of Supply for the 31st. Division, will proceed in the above mentioned train for embarkation in the H.T. MANITOU, for which complete berthing allotment is attached.

The 29th. Division details which went to Alexandria to embark in the NESSIAN will be sent to Port Said to join the MANITOU.

4. The chargers of officers proceeding on the MANITOU may be taken, and the chargers of all officers who proceeded on the LLANDOVERY CASTLE should also be taken.

5. Dinner will be the first meal issued on board ship on the day of embarkation. Details embarking should therefore have a breakfast ration with them.

6. Ten days' voyage rations will be embarked.

7. Four copies of nominal rolls of those embarking and four copies of special embarkation return will be required by the Embarkation Staff Officer.

P.N. Broadbent
Bt.Lt.Colonel,
For
Inspector General of Communications.

Cairo,
3rd. March, 1916.

Copies to ---
D.Q.M.G. G.H.Q.
D.A.G. 3rd. Ech.   D.N.T.O. ALEX.
G.O.C. 15th. Corps.   N.T.O. P.SAID.
G.O.C. 31st. Division.   G.O.C. 29th. Div.
G.O.C. ALEX.   D.R.T.
G.O.C. 9th. Corps.   D.A.D.R.T. ALEX. ISMAILIA. P.SAID.
Base Cdt. ALEX.   A.D.R.T. G.H.Q. ISMAILIA.
Adm.Cdt. P.SAID.   H. of B. F.E.
E.S.O. ALEX & P.SAID   D. of S. L.B.
P.N.T.O.
                                                    d

Details 29th Division & 31st Division to embark at Port Said,

5th March 1916.

ALLOTMENT OF BERTHING ACCOMMODATION

H. T. "MANITOU"

UNIT	Officers	O.Ranks	Horses.
Maximum Accommodation	60	1250	702
	~~2~~	~~879~~	30 off charges.
Advance Parties 29th Division.	3	57	
Supply Section train.	5	156	
86th Brigade	5	128	
87th "	7	167	
88th B "	3	235	
29th Div. Art.	1	95	
Royal Engineers.	1	39	
Divisional Sig. Sec.		2	
Div. Cyclists	1	13	
359th D.U.S.	1	78	
11th F. Bakery	1	20	
13th " "	3	33	
267. 227. 187 D.U.S.	1	35	
A.T. Cable Sect.	1	73	
95th F. Amb.	4	17	
94th Bde. H.Q.	10	180	
31st Divnl. Details.			
	52	1328	

P.

Following will entrain in a special train at SUEZ CAMP to-morrow night 4/5th for PORT SAID to embark in "MANITOU". Entrained at 1 AM & dep. 2.10 AM on 5th from SUEZ.

On arrival at PORT SAID, they will be joined on the "MANITOU" by the 15 officers 64 other ranks, Advance Party 29th Division, which left at 1730 on 2nd for Alexandria.

2/Lt G.H. Barker 24/5/15.	R.A.	1st Line Transport,	2 Officers	198 Other Ranks.
Lt Newenham R.M.F. /3/15	86th Brigade,	1st Line Transport Personnel,	2 Officers	156 O.R. 8 Grooms.
2/Lt T.E. Broodworth 1/Innis. Fus 17-12-14.	87th Brigade,	-do-	2 "	124 O.R. 8 Grooms.
Lt. A.G. Cardy 17-10-14 2/Hants	88th Brigade,	-do-	1 "	167 O.R. 9 Grooms.
Lt. J.K.B. Langley 8/12/12.	R.E.	-do-	1 "	95 O.R.
2/Lt Singleton - 15/1/15	Divnl. Signal Coy.,	-do-	1 "	39 O.R.
	Divnl. Cyclists,	-do-	-	2 O.R.

Officers Servants	9 Officers,	806 O.R. 9
Advance Party from Alexandria	9 Officers, 15 "	815 O.R. 64 O.R.
	24 Officers,	879 O.R.

and 30 Officers Chargers.
(10 from each Inf. Brigade.)

LIST OF OFFICERS PROCEEDING ON NIGHT 4/5 to PORT SAID
FOR EMBARKATION.
==

R.E.   Lieut. J.K.B. LANGLEY, R.E. in Command.

R.A.   { 2/Lt. G.H. Barker, R.F.A.
          { 2/Lt. H.R. Remington, R.F.A.

86th Bde. { Lieut. P.W. Newenham, R.M.F.
          { 2/Lt. T.R. Oxley, Dub. Fus.

87th Bde. { 2/Lt. T.E. Bloodworth, 1/Innsk. Fus.
          { 2/Lt. E.W. Cooke, 2/S.W.B.

88th Bde. Lieut. A.G. Cardy, 2/Hants.

Signal
    Coy. 2/Lt. C. Singleton.

"A" Form.
MESSAGES AND SIGNALS.
Army Form C. 2121A

Prefix	Code	m.	Words	Charge		No. of Message
Office of Origin and Service Instructions.					This message is on a/c of:	Recd. at 4 m.
			Sent			Date
			At	m.	Service.	From
			To			By
			By		(Signature of "Franking Officer.")	

TO: 86 Brigades DADOS
    87 "
    88 "

Sender's Number.	Day of Month	In reply to Number	
G.A 240.	3/3		A A A

The Lewis guns have now arrived and will be issued to units aaa 11500 rounds S.A.A. will be taken per Lewis Gun. aaa address all Bdes repeated DaDoS.

S. M. Capt. G.S.

From: 29th Div
Place:
Time: 1050.

The above may be forwarded as now corrected.   (Z)
Censor. Signature of Addressor or person authorised to telegraph in his name.
* This line should be erased if not required.

MESSAGES AND SIGNALS.

Service Instructions: ON CgM 23 H Co Ares

TO: DADOS 29th Divn

Sender's Number.	Day of Month.	In reply to Number.	AAA
OS 335	2/3	133	

GHQ have wired that 1500 rounds SAA should be taken per Lewis gun

FROM PLACE TIME: ADOS 9th Corps

COPY.

SECRET.

29th Division.

The D.A.D.O.S. 29th Division is arranging for the excess ammunition 18 pdr., 8928 rounds, that cannot be carried in battery or ammunition vehicles to be collected at Port Tewfik in boxes.

The port of embarkation is unknown to him or to me and so will you please arrange for this ammunition to be dispatched to the post of embarkation and placed on the ship which will convey the 1 Officer and 35 Other Ranks of the D.A.C. who will accompany the Division.

This ammunition will require a large amount of labour in manhandling and this method will obviate a congestion at the embarkation.

(Signed) C.H.Clark,
Major, R.A.
Brigade Major
for G.O.C. Commanding 29th Div. Artly.

B.M./3007
3d3d16.

2.

9th Corps.

Can the necessary arrangements be made, please? We will of course provide the labour, if local labour is not available for this work.

(Signed) C.G.Fuller,
Lieut.Col.

29th Division Headquarters.
3/3/16.

appx 4

(1-3)

OS. 352ª

OS. 352 (1)

In reply to B.M 30/ following just received from G.H.Q begins AAA 252 rounds per gun should be issued at SUEZ to 18 Pr Brigades of "29" Div. AAA Balance of 248 rounds per gun will be placed on board at ALEXANDRIA. AAA. Howitzer Batteries should draw to complete 200 rounds per howitzer at ALEXANDRIA ends.
 Wire Army number of rounds required to complete to 262 rounds per gun of ammunition and instruct Howitzer batteries to draw to complete to 200 rounds per howitzer at ALEXANDRIA AAA. Wire if all clear.

A.D.O.S.
9ª Corps.

O.S. 361

Appendix 4.

A.D.O.S. 9th Corps.

O.C.T. 4236   3rd.

In continuation of my O.C.T./4221 the 15th Bde. R.H.A. 17th and 147th Bdes R.F.A. are to take 450,000 rounds S.A.A. each with them aaa Levant Base has been asked to issue this ammunition to Bdes on application at Alexandria aaa Please issue necessary instructions.

   D.O.S. Medforce.

A.Q.M.G.

   For your information. All necessary instructions have been issued accordingly.

   Please return.

                 Sd. R.S.HAMILTON.
                                Lt. Col.
4/3/16   A.D.O.S. 9th Corps.

Headquarters,

   29th Division.

   For your information. This refers to my Q. 468 dated 3/3/16.

                 H. Needham

                 Lieut. Colonel.
4/3/16   for D.A.&.Q.M.G. 9th Corps.

(4005) Wt. W 1789-1402. 5 15. 48,000 Pads. S. B. Ltd.

"B" Form.

MESSAGES AND SIGNALS.

Army Form C 2122

(3)

Prefix	Code		Received	Sent	No. of Message
Office of Origin and Service Instructions.		Words.	At 2135 m.	At m.	Office Stamp.
Suez Camp		21	From 29	To	YB1 4.III.16
			By JM	By	T.B.L.

TO { 29ᵗ Divn

Sender's Number	Day of Month	In reply to Number	
1317/409	4		AAA

ADDS 9ᵗʰ Corps DS 361
4ᵗʰ Army DS 352 3ᵈ
received and action taken

From 29 DA
Place
Time

* This line should be erased if not required

Appx. 5

1—3

Secret

Appendix 5.

G.O.C. 9th Corps. Suez.

Following of 29th Division will embark at Alexandria on Wednesday 8th March.:-

17th Brigade R.F.A.
15th   "   R.H.A.

Part of 2/ South Wales Borderers and officers chargers of following :-

87th Brigade,
29th Divisional Headquarters
Divisional R.A. Headquarters.
     "   R.E.   "
Divisional Signal Company.

Ships Kingstonian and Huanchaco.

Orders with Train Timings and berthing allotments are being sent by special messenger to-night.

A.Q.M.G.
Savoy Hotel
CAIRO.

29th Division.

For information and necessary action.

6-3-16.

Lieutenant-Colonel,
for D.A. & Q.M.G.
9th Army Corps.

appx 6

1 — 4

Appendix 6.

C.R. 15534/Q/3.

The
General Officer Commanding

9th. Army Corps.
----

1. Attached please find train timings and berthing allotments for the first flight of 29th. Division, which consists of the following troops :

      17th. Brigade, R.F.A.
      15th. Brigade, R.F.A.
      Part 2nd. South Wales Borderers
and the Officers' chargers of 1st.K.O.S.B., 1st.Border Regt., 1st.Inniskilling Fus., 87th.Brigade Headquarters, 29th. Div. Headquarters, 29th.Div.Artillery Headquarters, 29th.Divisional Engineers Headquarters, Divisional Signal Company.

2. Embarkation will take place at Alexandria on March 8th. Train timings are arranged for the night of the 7th/8th. 8/9

3. Allotments must be adhered to as closely as possible. No alteration in train timings can be allowed.

4. Vehicles must be embarked as far as possible on the ship with the unit.

5. Ten days' voyage rations and forage will be embarked.

6. Officers and other ranks up to the full numbers given in the allotment form must be entrained for embarkation, any deficiency in numbers being made up from the 2nd.South Wales Borderers.

7. Tea will be the first meal issued on board ship on the day of embarkation. Units embarking should therefore have with them the unexpended portion of the day's rations.

8. Tents will not be taken.

9. Four copies of nominal roll of those embarking and four copies of special embarkation return will be required by the Embarking Staff Officer.

                                                                  Broadbent

Cairo,
6th. March, 1916.
                                          Bt.Lt.Colonel,
                                 For Inspector General of
                                    Communications.

Copies to ---
    D.Q.M.G. G.H.Q.   E.S.O. ALEX.
    D.A.G. 3rd.Ech.   D.R.T.
    G.O.C. 29th.Div.   A.D.R.T. G.H.Q. ISMAILIA.
    G.O.C. ALEX.   D.A.D.R.T. CAIRO?ALEX.& ISMAILIA.
    Base Cdt., ALEX.   H.of B. F.E.
    P.N.T.C.   D.of S. L.B.
    D.N.T.C. ALEX.

SECRET

ALLOTMENT OF BERTHING ACCOMMODATION.

15584/Q/3
Table 2.

29th. DIVISION.

1st. Flight, to embark ALEXANDRIA March 8th.

UNIT.	H.T. KINGSTONIAN					H.T. HUANCHACO.			
	Officers.	Other Ranks.	Horses.	Vehicles. 2-Wh.	4-Wh.	Officers.	Other Ranks.	Horses.	Vehicles. 2-W. 4-W.
Maximum Accommodation	37	1064	750			10	200	466	
17th. Brigade R.F.A.	19	395	562	96	1				
15th. Brigade R.F.A.	11	287	120	28	1	10	200	448	68
2nd. Sth. Wales Borderers	7	343	4						
1st. K. O. S. B.		4	4						
1st. Border Regiment		4	4						
1st. Inniskilling Fus.		4	4						
87th. Brigade Headquarters		4	4						
29th. Division Headquarters		6	8						
Hdqrs. Divisional Artillery		12	16						
Hdqrs. Divisional Engineers		2	2						
Divisional Signal Company		3	3						
	37	1064	731	124	2	10	200	448	68

d

C.R.15584/Q/3

General Officer Commanding,
9th Army Corps.

With reference to C.R.15584/Q/3 of today's date, on account of a mechanical breakdown of the Hired Transport "KINGSTONIAN" the move mentioned therein is postponed till further orders.

Cairo.
6th March 1916.

Bt. Lieut-Colonel,
for Inspector General of Communications.

Copies to D.Q.M.G.,G.H.Q.
        D.A.G.3rd Echelon.
        G.O.C.29th Division.
        G.O.C.Alexandria.
        Base Commdt.Alexandria.
        P.N.T.O.
        D.N.T.O.Alexandria.
        E.S.O.Alexandria.
        D.R.T.
        A.D.R.T.,G.H.Q.Ismalia.
        D.A.D.R.T.Cairo,Alex. and Ismailia.
        H.of B. Force in Egypt.
        D.of S. Levant Base.

C.R.15584/Q/3

General Officer Commanding,
9th Corps, Suez.

With reference to my C.R.15584/Q/3 of the 6th, the Hired Transports "KINGSTONIAN" and "HUANCHACO" will embark at Alexandria on the morning of the 9th of March.

Train timings and allotments are attached.

Cairo.
7th March 1916.

/for Bt.Lieut-Colonel,
for Inspector General of Communications.

Copies to D.Q.M.G.,G.H.Q.
        D.A.G.3rd Echelon.
        G.OC.29th Division.
        G.O.C.Alexandria.
        Base Commdt.Alexandria.
        P.N.T.O.
        D.M.T.O.Alexandria.
        E.S.O.Alexandria.
        D.R.T.
        A.D.R.T. G.H.Q.Ismailia.
        D.A.D.R.T.Cairo.Alex.Ismailia.
        H.of B. Force in Egypt.
        D.of S. Levant Base.

SECRET.

H.Q. 29th Division.

Please see attached wire from DAGLOCK, Cairo.

I understand from D.A.D.R.T., Suez that the programme will take place 24 hours later.

[signature]
Lieutenant-Colonel,
for D.A. & Q.M.G.
9th Army Corps.

7-3-1916.

15584/Q/3 & 4.

Train Allotment No 1.

MOVE OF
1st. Flight, 29th. DIVISION
From SUEZ to ALEXANDRIA

Unit.	Officers.	Other Ranks	Horses.
1st. Train, No. 834/701		~~158~~ 199	
17th. Brigade R. F. A.	7	~~160~~ ~~177~~	154
2nd. South Wales Borderers	3	114 ~~153~~ ~~147~~	
	10	313 ~~313~~	154
2nd. Train, No. 840/707			
17th. Brigade R.F.A.	6	130 ~~107~~ 165	150
2nd. South Wales Borderers	4	149 ~~188~~ ~~151~~	42
	10	314 ~~318~~ ~~341~~	15~~4~~ 2
3rd. Train, 802/711A.			
17th. Brigade R. F. A.	6	105 ~~117~~	59
15th. Brigade R. H. A.	5	~~206~~ ~~106~~ 194	95
	11	311 ~~313~~ ~~304~~	154
4th. Train, No.808/717A.		176	
15th. Brigade R. H. A.	8	129 ~~147~~	109
2nd. South Wales Borderers	10	98 137 ~~122~~	
1st. K. O. S. B.		42	42
1st. Border Regt.		4 x1	4 x1
1st. Royal Munster Fusiliers		4 x2	4 x2
87th. Brigade Headquarters		4	4
29th. Division Headquarters		6 1	8 1
Divisional R.A. Headquarters		12 4	16 15
Divisional R.E. Headquarters		2 3	2 3
Divisional Signal Company		3 2	3 2
	18	305 311	~~154~~ 147
5th. Train, No 814/827A		150 ~~167~~	
15th. Brigade R. H. A.	8	150	154
2nd. South Wales Borderers	~~10~~ 8	163	
	~~18~~ 16	313	154

1. As many vehicles as possible should be loaded on to each train.
2. The animals should be as closely packed as possible; all available space in the trains will be required for the personnel.
3. The Transport KINGSTONIAN, HUANCHACO and KAROA will be berthed close together at Alexandria Docks and on arrival of trains details should proceed to their allotted ship.

For TRAIN TIMINGS see Train Timings No 1.

C.R.15584/O/3 & 4.
Train Timing No.1.

TRAIN TIMINGS FOR THE MOVE OF 1ST FLIGHT 29TH DIVISION ON MARCH 8/9TH

No of Train	Type.	Loading Station.	Time train ready for loading.	Time leave loading Station.	Destination.	Arrive.
834/701	Cavalry.	SUEZ CAMP.	5.30.p.m.	7.30.p.m.	GABBARY DOCK.	5.40.a.m.
840/707	Cavalry.	SUEZ CAMP.	8.20.p.m.	10.20.p.m.	KINGSTONIAN.	8.45.a.m.
802/711.A.	Cavalry.	SUEZ CAMP.	11.10.p.m.	1.10.a.m.	KINGSTONIAN.	11.15.a.m.
808/717.A.	Cavalry.	SUEZ CAMP.	2.a.m.	4.10.a.m.	KINGSTONIAN.	2.30.p.m.
814/727.A.	Cavalry.	SUEZ CAMP.	5.a.m.	8.a.m.	HUANCHACO.	6.25.p.m.

M.P.

SECRET. Copy No. 1

OPERATION ORDER No. 22
by
MAJOR GENERAL H. de B. de Lisle. C.B., D.S.O.
Commanding 29th Division.

****

29th Divisional H.Q.
S U E Z.
7th March 1916.

1. The first portion of the first flight of the 29th Division for embarkation will be composed as follows, berthing allotments are attached, train timings will be forwarded when received.

    17th Brigade. R.F.A.
    15th Brigade. R.H.A.
    Part 2nd South Wales Borderers
    and officers' chargers of 2nd S.Wales Bdrs., 1st K.O.S.B., 1st Border Regt., 1st Inniskilling Fus., 87th Brigade H.Q., 29th Division H.Q., 29th Div.Artillery H.Q. 29th Divisional Engineers H.Q., Divisional Signal Co., 88th Brigade, 86th Brigade, R.E., Mobile Vet.Section.

2. Embarkation will probably take place at Alexandria on March 9th. Trains will probably leave Suez Camp, commencing at 1930 on 8th.

3. Allotments must be adhered to as closely as possible. No alteration in train timings can be allowed.

4. Vehicles must be embarked as far as possible on the ship with the unit.

5. Ten days' voyage rations and forage will be embarked.

6. Tea will be the first meal issued on board ship on the day of embarkation. Units should therefore have with them the unexpended portion of the Day's rations.

7. Tents will not be taken.

8. Four copies of nominal roll of those embarking and four copies of special embarkation return will be required by the Embarking Staff Officer.

C.S. Fuller.
Lieut.Colonel, G.S.
29th Division.

Issued at.....................

Copy No.
1. General Staff.
2. D.A.Q.M.G.
3. A.A. & Q.M.G.
4. C.R.A.
5. 86th Brigade
6. 87th   "
7. 88th   "
8. C.R.E.
9. Camp Commandant.
10. Officer i/c Signals.
11. 18th Mobile Vet. Section.
12. G.S.Office.
13.   "
14.   "

SECRET.

ALLOTMENT OF BERTHING ACCOMODATION.

29th Division.

1st Flight to embark Alexandria March 9th.

Unit.	H.M.T. "Kingstonian"					H.M.T. "Huauchaco".				
	Off.	O.R.	Horses.	Vehls. 2W/D	4W/D.	Off.	O.R.	Horses.	Vehls. 2W/D	4W
17th Brigade.R.F.A.	20	399	567	96	1	-	-	-	-	-
15th Brigade.R.H.A.	9	269	125	28	1	10	200	448	68	-
2/S.Wales Bdrers.	8	339	2	-	-	-	-	-	-	-
1/K.O.S.B.	-	2	2	-	-	-	-	-	-	-
1/Border Regt.	-	2	2	-	-	-	-	-	-	-
1/R.Innis. Fus.	-	1	1	-	-	-	-	-	-	-
87th Brigade. H.Q.	-	4	4	-	-	-	-	-	-	-
29th Div.H.Q.	-	1	1	-	-	-	-	-	-	-
H.Q.Div.Artillery.	-	4	4	-	-	-	-	-	-	-
H.Q.Div.Engineers.	-	3	3	-	-	-	-	-	-	-
Div. Signal Co..	-	2	2	-	-	-	-	-	-	-
88th Brigade.	-	6	6	-	-	-	-	-	-	-
86th Brigade.	-	5	5	-	-	-	-	-	-	-
R.E.	-	4	4	-	-	-	-	-	-	-
Mobile Vet. Section.	-	3	3	-	-	-	-	-	-	-
	37	1064	731	124	2	10	200	448	68	-

9th Army Corps.

1. Attached please find ~~train timings and berthing~~ allotments for H.T.KAROA, an additional ship to the first flight of the 29th Division.

The Units to be embarked are:-

Part of 57th Howitzer Brigade.
All remainder of 2nd South Wales Borderers.
No.64 Depot Unit of Supply, and
Detachment of 95th Field Ambulance (31st Division)
Records Sub Section and Base Depot (31st Division)

Of the above Units all are at Alexandria except 2nd S.W.B. at Suez.

2. Embarkation will take place at Alexandria on March 9th. Train timings are arranged for night of March 8/9th.

3. Allotments must be adhered to as closely as possible. No alteration in train timings can be allowed.

4. Vehicles must be embarked as far as possible on the ship with the Unit.

5. Ten days voyage rations and forage will be embarked.

6. Tea will be the first meal issued on board ship on the day of embarkation. Units embarking should therefore have with them the unexpended portion of the day's rations.

7. Tents will not be taken.

8. Four copies of nominal roll of those embarking and four copies of special embarkation return will be required by the Embarking Staff Officer.

9. As the only ships so far available are horse carrying ships it has been found impossible as regards artillery to adhere to paragraph one of letter C.M.Q.445, 26th February.

Bt.Lieut-Colonel,
for Inspector General of Communications.

Cairo,
March 7th, 1916.
Copies to:-
D.Q.M.G.,G.H.Q.
D.A.G.,3rd Ech.
G.O.C.15th Corps.
G.O.C.,29th Div.
G.O.C.,Alex.
Base Cmdt.,Alex.
P.N.T.O.
D.N.T.O.,Alex.
E.S.O.,Alex.
D.R.T.
A.D.R.T., G.H.Q.Ismailia.
D.A.D.R.T., Cairo,Alex, and Ismailia.
H.of B.,F.E.

M.P.

C.R.15995/9/4.

29th Division. 1st Flight to embark Alexandria, March 9th.

ALLOTMENT OF BERTHING ACCOMMODATION.

	H.T.KAROA.			Vehicles.	
UNIT.	Officers.	Other Ranks.	Horses.	2Wh.	4Wh.
Maximum Accommodation.	36	746	320		
57th Howitzer Bde.R.F.A.	13	315	320	x	x
South Wales Borderers.	20	300	-		
95th Field Ambulance.	1	73	-		
Records and Base Depot.	2	40	-		
64th Depot Unit of Supply.	1	13	-		
TOTAL	37	741	320		

x As many as possible according to capacity.

M.P.

"C" Form (Original).
Army Form C. 2123.
MESSAGES AND SIGNALS. No. of Message

Prefix	Code	Words	Received	Sent, or sent out	Office Stamp.
	£ s. d.		From Copy	At	7.III.16.
Charges to collect			By	m.	
Service Instructions.				To	
				By	

Handed in at 160 M Phone Office m. Received m.

TO 29th Division   Copy of message addressed A.A.& Q.M.G. 9th Corps

*Sender's Number	Day of Month	In reply to Number		AAA
The	move	of	troops	29th
Divn	from	Suez	Camp	will
commence	tomorrow	night	8th	inst
by	five	trains	1st	train
depart	Suez	Camp.	7.20 p.m	2nd
train	10.10 p.m	3rd	train	1.0 a.m
4th	train	4 am	5th	train
7.50 am				

FROM PLACE & TIME Da DRT

A.Q.M.G.

IXth Corps.

The composition of a Cavalry Train is as follows:-

1	1st Class	24 seats.
1	2nd Class	32 "
4	3rd Class	192 "
18	Animal Trucks (covered)	162 - 180 animals
2	30 ton box trucks.	60 tons capacity.
6	Flat trucks	90 " "
1	Goods brake	8 " "
1	Brake Post and Luggage	8 " "

To take 1 Squadron of Cavalry or 1 Battery R.A. length of train, including engine, 324 metres.

Suez Docks.
7th March, 1916.

Sd. R.S. Milward. Capt.
R.T.O.

29th Division.

For information.

7/3/16.

Lieut. Colonel.
for D.A & Q.M.G. 9th Corps.

appx 7

"A" Form.
MESSAGES AND SIGNALS.
Army Form C.2121

Prefix	Code	m.	Words	Charge	This message is on a/c of :	Recd. at	m.
Office of Origin and Serv. Instructions.			Sent			Date	
Priority			At	m.	Service.	From	
— do			To			By	
			By		(Signature of "Franking Officer.")		

TO { H.Q.M.G. Cairo
9th Corps.

Sender's Number	Day of Month	In reply to Number	AAA
* A.B. 472	8/3		

Reference ~~your~~ C.R. 15584/Q/4 There will be 19 officers and 400 O.R. of the SWB remaining and not 20 officers and 300 O.R. as in the above table aaa Please wire if the extra hundred O.R. can be sent for embarkation on H.T. KAROA on 9th inst. aaa The difference in figures is ~~~~ owing to an Artillery draft having arrived at the last moment and being sent on KINGSTONIAN vice equivalent number S.W. Borderers. aaa addressed A.Q.M.G. Cairo repeated 9th Corps.

From 29th Div.
Place
Time 1000

The above may be forwarded as now corrected. (Z)

"C" Form (Duplicate).   Army Form C. 2123.
MESSAGES AND SIGNALS.
No. of Message

| Service Instructions | (New) Priority CA | Charges to Pay. £ s. d. | Office Stamp. 6.11.15 |

Handed in at _____ Office 11.50 m. Received 12.15 m.

TO 29th Dn

Sender's Number	Day of Month	In reply to Number	AAA
448A		WB 472	

Send the extra hundred men by passenger train leaving Suez 5.25 pm tonight and 7 am tomorrow arranging details locally with railtof aaa the South Wales Borderers will be accommodated on ship at expense of 57th Howitzer Bde addressed 29th Divn repeated 9th Corps

FROM Daglork
PLACE & TIME

"C" Form (Duplicate).
MESSAGES AND SIGNALS.
Army Form C. 2123.
No. of Message

		Charges to Pay. £ s. d.	Office Stamp.
	109 GO Ollive		

Service Instructions.

Handed in at GO Office 2050 m. Received 2107 m.

TO 29 Divn

Sender's Number	Day of Month	In reply to Number	AAA
GN 888	8/3		

Following received by telephone from DAGLOCK aaa Begins aaa No 4486 8/3/16 aaa With reference to my 4484 and 4485 the following message has been sent to embarking staff officer alexandria aaa Begins aaa 29th Div artillery for huanchaco and Korea have received an extra 100 men since berthing arrangements were issued aaa Kindly arrange the embarkation of these vessels so that only portion of 57th Brigade remains behind aaa All other units allotted must be completely embarked aaa The additional 100 men will

FROM
PLACE & TIME

"C" Form (Duplicate).   Army Form C. 2123.
MESSAGES AND SIGNALS.   No. of Message.

Charges to Pay.   Office Stamp.

Service Instructions.

Handed in at _____ Office 2051 m. Received 2107 m.

TO

Sender's Number | Day of Month | In reply to Number | A A A

Travel by passenger train 5.25 pm tonight and 7 am tomorrow from SUEZ to ALEXANDRIA aaa Ends aaa

FROM PLACE & TIME: 9/Corps 2050

"A" Form.
MESSAGES AND SIGNALS.
Army Form C. 2121.

Prefix	Code	m.	Words	Charge	This message is on a/c of:	Recd. at _____ m.
Office of Origin and Service Instructions.		Sent				Date _____
Priority		At _____ m.			Service.	From _____
		To _____				
		By _____		(Signature of "Franking Officer.")	By _____

TO { G.O.C. Alexandria
9th Corps

| Sender's Number | Day of Month | In reply to Number | AAA |
| AC 173 | 8/3 | | |

Reference I.G.C. No 15854/Q/4 and attached table I presume you will take necessary action as regards 57 Howitzer Brigade aaa Please note that the 315 other ranks in the above table will be reduced to 215 by Daglish's wire No 4484 of today aaa addressed G.O.C. Alexandria repeated 9th Corps.

From 29th Div
Place
Time 1310

"A" Form.
Army Form C. 2121.
MESSAGES AND SIGNALS.

Prefix......Code......m.	Words	Charge	This message is on a/c of:	Recd. at......m.
Office of Origin and Service Instructions.				
Priority	Sent			Date......
Do	At......m.		Service.	From......
	To......			
	By......		(Signature of "Franking Officer.")	By......

TO { RTO Suez Docks
     G Corps

Sender's Number	Day of Month	In reply to Number	AAA
AB 174	8/3		

Following from Daglock begins Send the extra hundred men by passenger train leaving Suez 5.25 pm tonight and 7am tomorrow arranging details locally with Railoff ends aaa Please inform me by telephone urgently number to go by each train aaa address RTO Suez Docks repeated G Corps.

D.M. Capt
JS

From 74th Div
Place
Time 1455

SECRET.

Headquarters,
    87th Brigade.

Attached please find extracts from orders issued by I.G.C., dated 7th March 1916.

Herewith Train Timings referred to in Para. 1 Operation Order No. 22 dated 7th March 1916. Please acknowledge by wire.

8th March 1916.

Lieut. Col. G.S.
29th Division.

The Units to be embarked are :-

All remainder of 2nd South Wales Borderers.

Embarkation will take place at Alexandria on March 9th. Train timings are arranged for night March 8/9th.

Vehicles must be embarked as far as possible on the ship with the unit.

Ten days voyage rations and forage will be embarked.

Tea will be the first meal issued on board ship on the day of embarkation. Units embarking should therefore have with them then unexpended portion of the day's rations.

Tents will not be taken.

Four copies of nominal roll of those embarking and four copies of special embarkation return will be required by the Embarking Staff Officer.

29th Division.   1st Flight to embark Alexandria, March 9th.

ALLOTMENT OF BERTHING ACCOMMODATION.

H.T. KAROA.

Unit.	Off.	O.R.	Horses	Vehicles. 2 W.	4 W.
Maximum Accommodation	36	746	320		
57th How. Bde. R.F.A.	13	315	320	x	x
South Wales Borderers	20	300	-		
95th Field Ambulance	1	73	-		
Records & Base Depot	2	40	-		
64th Depot Unit of Supply	1	13	-		
	37	741	320		

x   As many as possible according to capacity.

Herewith Train Timings referred to in Para. 1
Operation Order No. 22 dated 7th March 1916.

Please acknowledge receipt by wire.

for

Lieut. Colonel, G.S.

8th March 1916.

29th Division.

15584/Q/3 24.
Train Allotment No. 1.

Move of
1st Flight, 29th Division
From SUEZ to ALEXANDRIA

Unit	Off.	O.R.	Horses
1st Train, No. 834/701.			
17th Bde. R.F.A.	7	199	154
2nd South Wales Borderers	3	114	
	10	313	154
2nd Train, No. 840/707			
17th Bde. R.F.A.	6	165	150
2nd South Wales Borderers	4	149	2
	10	314	152
3rd Train, No. 802/711A			
17th Bde. R.F.A.	6	117	59
15th Bde. R.H.A.	5	194	95
	11	311	154
4th Train, No. 808/717A			
15th Bde. R.H.A.	8	176	109
2nd South Wales Borderers	10	98	
1st K.O.S. Borderers		2	2
1st Border Regt.		1	1
1st Royal Innis. Fusiliers		2	2
87th Brigade Headquarters		4	4
29th Divisional Headquarters		1	1
Divisional R.A. Headquarters		4	5
Divisional R.E. Headquarters		3	3
Divisional Signal Co.		2	2
88th Brigade		6	6
86th Brigade		5	5
R.E.		4	4
Mobile Veterinary Section		3	3
	18	311	147
5th Train, No. 814/727A			
15th Bde. R.H.A.	8	150	154
2nd South Wales Borderers	8	163	
	16	313	154

1. As many vehicles as possible should be loaded on to each train.
2. The animals should be as closely packed as possible; all available space in the trains will be required for the personnel.
3. The Transport KINGSTONIAN, HUANCHACO and KAROA will be berthed close together at ALEXANDRIA DOCKS and on arrival of trains details should proceed to their allotted ships.

For TRAIN TIMINGS see Train Timings No. 1.

C.R. 15584/Q/3 & 4.
Train Timing No. 1.

TRAIN TIMINGS FOR THE MOVE OF 1ST FLIGHT 29TH DIVISION ON MARCH 8/9th.

No. of Train	Type	Loading Station	Time train ready for loading	Time leave loading station	Destination	Arrive.
					GABBARY DOCK	
834/701	Cavalry	SUEZ CAMP	5.30 pm.	7.30 pm.	KINGSTONIAN	5.40 am.
840/707	Cavalry	SUEZ CAMP	8.20 pm.	10.20 pm.	KINGSTONIAN	8.45 am.
802/711 A	Cavalry	SUEZ CAMP	11.10 pm.	1.10 am.	KINGSTONIAN	11.15 am.
808/717 A	Cavalry	SUEZ CAMP	2.0 am.	4.10 am.	KINGSTONIAN	2.30 pm.
815/727 A	Cavalry	SUEZ CAMP	5.0 am.	8.0 am.	HUANCHACO	6.25 pm.

appx 8

1-5

15584/Q/5.

Appendix 8.

It has not been found possible to complete Train Timings and Train Allotments for moves on night of 10th./11th. March to accompany these orders.

These will be issued tomorrow morning, the 9th. instant.

(Sd) R.M.,
For I. G. C.

)))------------(((

d

C.R.15584/Q/5.

The

General Officer Commanding

9th. ARMY CORPS.

FIRST FLIGHT, 29th. DIVISION (Continued).

---

1. Attached please find train timings and berthing allotments for the First Flight of the 29th. Division on the Hired Transports MEGANTIC, ELELE and WANDILLA.

2. The MEGANTIC will embark at PORT SAID on March 11th.

   The ELELE will embark at ALEXANDRIA on March 11th.

   The WANDILLA will embark at SUEZ on March 10th.

3. Units to be embarked are :

   87th.Infantry Brigade Headquarters.
   1st.K.O.S.B.
   1st.Royal Inniskilling Fusiliers
   Portion Machine Gun Coy.,87th.Brigade
   Remainder 57th.Howitzer Brigade.
   Portion 147th. Brigade,R.F.A.
   Chaplains 87th.Brigade.

   Of the above all are at SUEZ, except portion 57th.Howitzer Brigade at Alexandria.

4. The whole of the 147th.Bde.,R.F.A. will be railed to Alexandria. Paras. 3 to 9 of my letter C.R. 15584/Q/4 will apply to this embarkation.

Cairo,
8th.March,1916.

For
Bt.Lt.Colonel,
Inspector General of Communications.

Copies to ---

D.Q.M.G. G.H.Q.	E.S.O. ALEX.
D.A.G.3rd.Ech.	E.S.O. PORT SAID.
G.O.C. 15th.Corps (For information only)	E.S.O. SUEZ.
	D.R.T.
G.O.C. 29th.Div.	A.D.R.T. ISMAILIA.
G.O.C. ALEX.	D.A.D.R.T. CAIRO.
Base Cdt.,ALEX.	D.A.D.R.T. ALEX.
Base Cdt., SUEZ	D.A.D.R.T. ISMAILIA.
Base Cdt.,PORT SAID.	D.A.D.R.T. SUEZ.
P.N.T.C.	R.T.O. SUEZ.
D.N.T.O. ALEX.	R.T.O. PORT SAID.
N.T.O. PORT SAID.	H.of B. F.E.
N.T.O. SUEZ.	D.of S. L.B.

29th DIVISION 1st FLIGHT CONTINUED.

C.R.15584/Q/5.
Table 4.

ALLOTMENT OF BERTHING ACCOMMODATION.

TO EMBARK AT	PORT SAID 11th March. H.T. "MEGANTIC"			ALEXANDRIA 11th March. H.T. "EVELE"			SUEZ 10th March. H.T. "WANDILLA"		
	Off.	O.R.	Horses	Off.	O.R.	Horses	Off.	O.R.	Horses.
Maximum Accommodation.	101	1897		16	500	550	100	1343	-
57th Howitzer Bde. R.F.A.			37 34	12	200	238			
147th Bde. R.F.A.				4	300	312			
87th Inf. Bde. H.Qrs.	3						29 23	596	
1st K.O.S.B's	10	368					30 31	699 721	
1st R.Inniskilling Fs.							4 1	48 26	
87th Bde Machine Gun Coy.							3 2		
Chaplains 87th Bde.									
TOTAL				16	500	550	57	1343	-

Note: As from [illegible]. Main lines and trans allotment [illegible] be forwarded later.

C.R. 15584/Q/5.

The

    General Officer Commanding

        9th. CORPS.

Herewith Train Timings to be attached to my C.R. 15584/Q/5 of to-day's date.

                                              Bt.Lt.Colonel,
                                   For
Cairo,   Inspector General of
   8th.March,1916.   Communications.

                                                                           d

C.R. 15584/Q/5.
Train Allotment No.2.

MOVE OF 1st.FLIGHT, 29th.DIVISION (Continued)
on night 10th/11th.March,1916.

Unit.	Officers.	Other Ranks	Horses.
1st.Train, No.834/701.			
147th. Brigade, R. F. A.	10	255	176
2nd. Train, No.840/707.			
147th. Brigade, R.F.A.	10	254	176
3rd. Train, No.802/801.			
87th. Inf. Brigade Headquarters	3	37	—
1st. K.O.S.B.	10	368	—
	13	405	—

1. All guns and vehicles will be loaded on the two Cavalry Trains. An extra flat truck will be attached to each to enable this to be done.

2. On arrival at Alexandria Docks the part of the 147th.Brigade R.F.A. not for embarkation will proceed by march route to the Embarkation Rest Camp.

Ra.

For TRAIN TIMINGS see Train Timings No 2.

d

-----oOo-----

G.R. 15584/C/5.
Train Timings No 2.

TRAIN TIMINGS FOR THE MOVE OF FIRST FLIGHT, 29th.DIVISION (Continued) ON NIGHT 10th/11th.MARCH,1916.

No of Train	Type	Loading Station	Time train ready for loading	Time leave loading Station	Destination	Arrive
834/7C1	Cavalry	SUEZ CAMP	5.30 p.m.	7.30 p.m.	GABBARY DOCKS H.T. ELELE	5.40 a.m.
840/707	Cavalry	SUEZ CAMP	8.20 p.m.	10.20 p.m.	H.T. ELELE	8.45 a.m.
802/801	Emergency	SUEZ CAMP	11.10 p.m.	1.10 a.m.	DCRT SAID. H.T. MEGANTIC	7.15 a.m.

For TRAIN ALLOTMENTS see Train Allotments No 2.

Summary of Cipher message
4490 8/3.

Wandilla

		off	OR
March 10th	1 KOSB.	20	596
Suez	Innis Fus.	30	699
	87th Bde M.G. Coy	4	48
	Chaplain	3	

Megantic.

		off	OR
March 11th	KOSB. Remainder i.e.	10	368
Port Said.	87th I.B. HQ.	3	37

In the event of Batt'n figures varying, the numbers of the B.M.G. Coy sh'd be varied according-ly. PORT SAID numbers must be adhered to.

Train timings follow by 11 train to-day.

9/6/16.

	off	OR
KOSB.s	30	964

	Actual Strength.		Diff'ce for embarkation	
	O/r.	O.R.	O/r	
1 KOSB.	33	—	964	+3	nil.
1 Innis. Fus.	31.	—	721	+1	+22
M.Gun Coy.	8.	—	137		
Chaplains.	4.			(+1)	
~~KOSB~~					
87 B.HQ.	3	—	34.	nil	−3

Readjusted figures for embarkation.

		O/r	O.R.
Wandilla	1 KOSB.	23	— 596.
	1 Innis. Fus	31	— 721
Suez.	87° B. H.Q.C.	1	— 26.
10ᵗʰ	Chaplains.	3	
Megantic	KOSB.	10	368.
P. Said.	87° B.HQ	3	34
11ᵗʰ			

MESSAGES AND SIGNALS.

Army Form C. 2121.

No. of Message _____

Prefix _____ Code _____ m. Words | Charge
Office of Origin and Service Instructions.

This message is on a/c of:

Recd. at ③ m.
Date
From
By

Sent At _____ m.
To _____
By _____

(Signature of "Franking Officer.")

TO { G.O.C. Alexandria.
     9th Corps.

Sender's Number: AB479
Day of Month: 9/3.
In reply to Number:
AAA

Reference CR 15584/Q/5 and attached table it is presumed you are taking action as regards the men of 57th Howitzer Brigade RFA. aaa addressed GOC Alexandria repeated 9th Corps.

D. M. Copp
/H

From: 29th Div.
Place:
Time: 1307.

"C" Form (Original). Army Form C. 2123.
MESSAGES AND SIGNALS.

Prefix	Code	Words	Received	Sent, or sent out	Office Stamp
	£ s. d.		From	At m.	9.III.16
Charges to collect			By	To	
Service Instructions				By	
via Alexandria					

Handed in at _____ Office 2045 m. Received 2159 m.

TO 29th Div Suez

*Sender's Number	Day of Month	In reply to Number	AAA
A31233	9th	Your ab 479	

action being taken*

FROM
PLACE & TIME Serial

Deputy Director of Remounts.

With reference to your demand for railway transport for 326 horses to Alexandria to embark on hired transport KAROA, please note that an animal train has been arranged for to-night 8th/9th March as follows:-

    Entraining Station   - Abbassia Siding.
    Train ready for loading   - 8 p.m.
    Time leave loading station   - 10.15 p.m.
    Time arrive Alexandria Docks - 4.45 a.m.

(sd) A.C.W. Clayton Captain,

Cairo,
8th March, 1916.
                    for A.Q.M.G., FORCE IN EGYPT.

Copies to:- G.H.Q. M.E.F.
          G.O.C. 9th Corps,
          G.O.C. 29th Divn.
          D.R.T.
          D.A.D.R.T. Alex.
          R.T.O. Cairo,
          H. of B. F. in E.
          D. of S. L.B.

F.B.P.

87th Brigade.
Divisional Artillery.

      Attached please find copy of orders received from I.G.C. under date 8th March 1916.

                                                                Lieut.Colonel, G.S.
9th March 1916.   29th Division

COPY.

C.R.15584/Q/5.

The
    General Officer Commanding,
        9th Army Corps.

FIRST FLIGHT, 29th Division (Continued).

1. Attached please find train timings and berthing allotments for the First Flight of the 29th Division on the Hired Transports MEGANTIC, ELELE and WANDILLA.

2. The MEGANTIC will embark at Port SAID on March 11th.

    The ELELE will embark at ALEXANDRIA on March 11th.

    The WANDILLA wil embark at SUEZ on March 10th.

3. Units to be embarked are:

    87th Infantry Brigade Headquarters.
    1st K.O.S.B.
    1st R. Inniskilling Fusiliers.
    Portion Machine Gun Coy., 87th Brigade.
    Remainder 57th Howitzer Brigade.
    Portion 147th Brigade., R.F.A.
    Chaplains 87th Brigade.

Of the above all are at SUEZ, except portion 57th Howitzer Brigade at Alexandria.

4. The whole of the 147th Brigade, R.F.A. will be railed to Alexandria, Paras. 3 to 9 of my letter C.R. 15584/Q/4 will apply to this embarkation.

(Signed) R. MAINWARING
Capt.
for Bt.Lt.Colonel,
For
Inspector General of Communications.

Cairo,
8th March 1916.

C.R.1584/Q/5.
Table 4.

29th DIVISION 1st FLIGHT CONTINUED.

ALLOTMENT OF BERTHING ACCOMODATION.

TO EMBARK AT	PORT SAID 11th March. H.T."MEGANTIC".			ALEXANDRIA 11th March. H.T."ELELE".			SUEZ 10th March. H.T."WANDILLA".		
	Off.	O.R.	Horses.	Off.	O.R.	Horses.	Off.	O.R.	Horses.
Maximum Accomodation.	101	1897		16	500	550	100	1343	1343
57th Howitzer Bde.R.F.A.				12	200	258			
147th Bde.R.F.A.				4	3000	312			
87th Inf.Bde.H.Qrs.	3	34					23	596	
1st K.O.S.B.	10	368					31	707	
1st R.Innls. Fus.							1	40	
87th Bde Machine Gun Coy.							2		
Chaplains 87th Bde.									
TOTAL				16	500	550	57	1343	

Note. Train timings and train allotments will be forwarded later.

Paras. 3 to 9 referred to in para 4 of C.R.15584/Q/5.

3. Allotments must be adhered to as closely as possible. No alteration in train timings can be allowed.

4. Vehicles must be embarked as far as possible on the ship with the unit.

5. Ten days voyage rations and forage will be embarked.

6. Tea will be the first meal issued on board ship on the day of embarkation. Units embarking should therefore have with them the unexpended portion of the day's rations.

7. Tents will not be taken.

8. Four copies of nominal roll of those embarking and four copies of special embarkation return will be required by the Embarking Staff Officer.

9. As the only ships so far available are horse carrying ships it has been found impossible as regards artillery to adhere to paragraph one of letter C.M.Q.445, 26th February.

App x 9

1 - 4

SECRET

87th Brigade.
C.R.E.
A.D.M.S.
18th Mobile Vet. Section.

Herewith orders received from I.G.C. for your information and compliance. Instructions regarding times of embarkation, and conveyance of baggage will be issued later.

(notes as below)

C. Fuller
Lieut Colonel, G.S.
29th Division.

10th March 1916.

87" Bde — Refre. para 3, the chargers as shewn below have been applied for to complete your Bde.

87" Bde H.Q.	3
2nd SWB	6
1/ KOSB	6
1/ R. I. Fus.	6
1/ Border Regt.	6
Machine Gun Coy.	9
	36

CRE — Refre para 3, 7 additional horses have been applied for to complete the London Fd Co. in chargers.

ADMS — Refre para 3, 10 additional chargers have been applied for to complete 88" Fd. Ambce.

COPY.　　　　　　　　　　　　　　　　　　　　　　　C.R. 15584/Q/6.

SECRET.

The General Officer Commanding,

    9th Corps,

        Suez.

FIRST FLIGHT 29th DIVISION (continued).

1. The Hired Transport WARILDA having become available is added to the 1st flight.

2. The following units will embark at Suez on the 11th instant:-

    1st Battn. Border Regt.
    Machine Gun Co. 87th Brigade (less numbers embarked on WARILDA)
    88th Field Ambulance.
    18th Mobile Veterinary Section.
    2nd London Field Co. R.E.

    Numbers 192, 203, 235, and 358 Depot Units of Supply will embark at Port Said being concentrated there on the 11th instant.

3. Sufficient personnel (i.e.:- 1 man to each pair of animals) of the units in possession of horses to be embarked, must be left behind to be embarked at a later date.

4. Embarkation orders previously issued will apply.

                                (sgd.) R.Mainwaring, Ca

Cairo,   for Bt. Lieut-Colonel,

  March 9th 1916.   for Inspector General of Communicatio

"A" Form.   Army Form C. 2121.

MESSAGES AND SIGNALS.   No. of Message _____

Prefix ___ Code ___ m.	Words	Charge	This message is on a/c of:	Recd. at ___ m.
Office of Origin and Service Instructions.	Sent			Date
	At ___ m.		Service.	From
	To			By
	By		(Signature of "Franking Officer.")	

TO {

| Sender's Number | Day of Month | In reply to Number | **AAA** |

arrange direct with OC Train with regard
to the Transport they require and the
times they require it aaa addressed
Border Regt 87th Bde M G Coy, A.D.M.S.
88 Field Ambulance 18 Mobile Veterinary
Section C.R.E. repeated A.D.M.S. O C Train

D. O'Ryley
JS

From 29th DW
Place
Time 1935

The above may be forwarded as now corrected.   (Z)

Censor.   Signature of Addressor or person authorized to telegraph in his name

* This line should be erased if not required.

"C" Form (Duplicate). Army Form C. 2123.
MESSAGES AND SIGNALS. No. of Message...........

Service Instructions.	Charges to Pay. £ s. d.	Office Stamp.
	Prio	YB1 10.III.16
	H.O.O. 1626	

Handed in at .... Office ......m. Received ......m.

TO 29th Devon Suez Camp

| Sender's Number | Day of Month 16 | In reply to Number | AAA |

R.J. Embarkation tomorrow aaa Border Regiment should arrive noon other details two from aaa officers selected for ships adjutant steps 5m ships to H.S. band six other ranks should report embarkation office ten am bringing with them nominal rolls in duplicate and embarkation state for all troops embarking

Embarking Suez Docks

FROM
PLACE & TIME

C.R.15584/Q/7.

SECRET.

General Officer Commanding,
    9th Corps, Suez.

SECOND FLIGHT 29TH DIVISION.

1. Attached please find berthing allotment for the Hired Transport "MENOMINEE" which will embark at Alexandria on the 12th March.

2. Units to be embarked are:-

    Remainder 147th Brigade R.F.A.
    Artillery reinforcements (excluded from "KINGSTONIAN" and "KAROA"
    Divisional Signal Company.   )
    Divisional Engineers H.Qrs.   )   AT SUEZ.
    1st Royal Dublin Fusiliers.   )
    Remainder horses 29th Division.   )

3. Train timings will be telegraphed to all concerned for the units now at Suez.

4. The orders previously issued will apply.

Cairo.
10th March 1916.

Captain.
D.A.Q.M.G.
for Inspector General of Communications.

Copies to D.Q.M.G., G.H.Q.
    D.A.G. 3rd Echelon.
    G.O.C. 29th Division.
    G.O.C. Alexandria Dist.
    Base Commdt. Alex.
    Base Commdt. Suez.
    P.N.T.O.
    D.N.T.O. Alexandria.
    E.S.O. Alexandria.
    D.R.T.
    A.D.R.T. Ismailia.
    D.A.D.R.T. Cairo Alex. Ismailia and Suez.
    R.T.O. Suez.
    H. of B. Force in Egypt.
    D. of S. Levant Base.

C.R.15584/Q/7.
Table 6.

ALLOTMENT OF BERTHING ACCOMODATION.

2ND FLIGHT 29TH DIVISION.

TO EMBARK AT ALEXANDRIA 12TH MARCH.

Unit.	Hired Transport "MENOMINEE"		
Maximum Accomodation	Officers. 60	Other ranks 1154	Horses. 640
147th Brigade R.F.A.	16	209	250
Remaining horses 29th Divn-		36	60 or less
Artillery Reinforcements.	-	100	- X
Divnl. Sig. Company.	6	163	-
1st Royal Dublin Fusrs.	27	659	-
Divnl. Engineers H.Qrs.	3	9	-
TOTAL.	52	1175	310

X Excluded from "KAROA" and "KINGSTONIAN"

TELEPHONE MESSAGE FROM 9TH CORPS
10/3/16.

Embarkation takes place on the 12th.   Units to be
embarked, remainder of 147th Brigade R.F.A.; 100 Artillery
Reinforcements; Divisional Signal Co.,; Divisional H.Q., R.E.;
remainder of the Horses of the Division.   Two trains will
be run, each having a capacity of 520 men with proportionate
number of Firsts.   Each train will accomodate 40 Animals.
The first train is timed to be ready for loading 5.30 p.m.
11/3/16.

SECRET.

Officer i/c Signals
C.R.E.
86th Brigade.
Camp Commandant.
88th Brigade.

The following will embark to-morrow on the
"MENOMINEE" at Alexandria.

    Divisional Signal Co.
    Divisional Engineers H.Q.
    1st Dublin Fusiliers.
    Remainder of horses 29th Division.

These troops will entrain this evening in two Infantry trains, the first starting from Suez Camp at 1930, the second at 2220.

Train allotment will follow as soon as possible. There will be ample accommodation.

A copy of allotment of Berthing Accommodation is attached.

                                              Lieut. Colonel, GS.
11th March 1916.   29th Division.

C.R.15584/Q/7.
Table 6.

ALLOTMENT OF BERTHING ACCOMODATION.

2nd FLIGHT 29th DIVISION.

TO EMBARK AT ALEXANDRIA 12th MARCH.

Unit.	Hired Transport "MENOMINEE"		
Maximum Accomodation	Officers.	Other Ranks	Horses
	60	1154	640
147th Brigade, R.F.A.	16	209	250
Remaining Horses 29th Div.	–	35	60 or less
Artillery Reinforcements.	–	100	– X
Divisional Signal Company.	6	163	–
1st Royal Dublin Fus.	27	659	–
Divnl. Engineers H.Qrs.	3	9	–
TOTAL.	52	1175	310

X Excluded from "KAROA" and "KINGSTONIAN".

C.R.15584/Q/7.
Train Timing No.3.

The General Officer Commanding,

9th Corps.

The following are train timings for the move ordered in my letter numbered as above of todays date:-

First Train.

   Type..................Infantry.
   Ready for loading at Suez Camp at 5.30.p.m., 11th.
   Leave at..............7.30.p.m.
   Timing No.............834/701.
   Arrive Gabbary Docks....5.40.a.m.

Second Train.

   Type..........................Infantry.
   Ready for loading at Suez Camp at 8.20.p.m., 11th.
   Leave at......................10.20.p.m.
   Timing No.....................840/707.
   Arrive Gabbary Docks..........8.45.p.m.

Mainwaring
Captain,

Cairo,

  March 10th, 1916.   for Inspector General of
              Communications.

Copies to:-
  D.Q.M.G., G.H.Q.
  D.A.G., 3rd Echelon.
  G.O.C., 29th Division.
  G.O.C., Alexandria Dist.
  Base Cmdt. Alex.
  Base Cmdt. Suez.
  P.N.T.O.
  D.N.T.O., Alexandria.
  E.S.O., Alex.
  D.R.T.
  A.D.R.T., Ismailia.
  D.A.D.R.T., Cairo, Alex, Ismailia, and Suez.
  R.T.O., Suez.
  H.of B., Force in Egypt.
  D.of S., Levant Base.

86th & 88th Brigades.
C.R.E.
Camp Commandant.
Signals.

In continuation of C.G.S. 12 of to-day's date, herewith Train Timings and Allotment referred to therein.

11th March 1916.

Lieut. Colonel, G.S.
29th Division.

TRAIN ALLOTMENT.

Unit	Officers	Other Ranks	Horses
1st Train No. 834/701.			
R.Dublin Fus.	17	422	1
R.E. Headquarters.	3	9	
29th Divisional H.Q.		6	8
88th Brigade H.Q.		4	4
R.Munster Fus .		1	1
Lancs. Fus .		1	1
	20	443	15
2nd Train No. 840/707.			
R.Dublin Fus.	10	237	
Divisional Signal Co.	7	193	
88th Brigade.		18	18
	17	448	18

C.R. 15584/Q/7.

TRAIN TIMINGS.   MARCH 11th 1916.

	No. of Train.	Type.	Loading Station.	Time train ready for loading.	Time leave loading Station.	Destination	Arrive.
1st Train	834/701	Infantry	Suez Camp	1730	1930	Alexandria	0540
2nd Train.	840/707	Infantry	Suez Camp	2020	2220	Alexandria	0845

appx 10

1-3

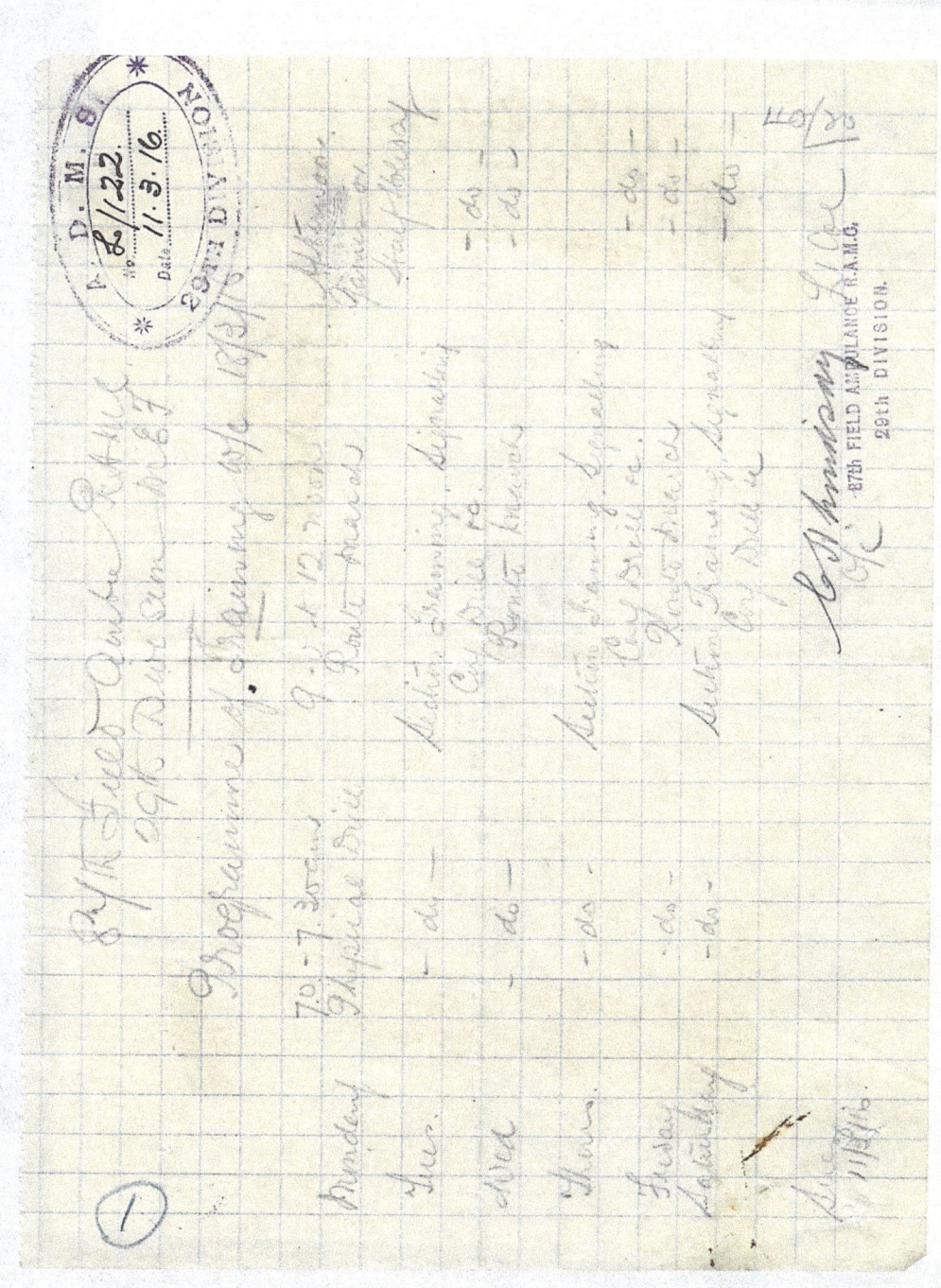

87/R Field Amb: R.A.M.C.
C/o D.H. Q. 29th Div: A.M. 27

A.D.M.S.
No. 2/1/22.
Date 11.3.16.
29th DIVISION

Programme of Training w/e 18/3/16

Monday	7.0 – 7.30am Physical Drill	9. to 12 noon Route March	afternoon Tent pitching
Tues.	– do –	Indoor Squad drill. Signalling	– do –
Wed.	– do –	Co. Drill etc	– do –
		Tent pitching	
Thurs.	– do –	Section training Signalling	– do –
		Coy Drill etc	
Friday	– do –	Route march	– do –
Saturday	– do –	Section Training Signalling	– do –
		by sec.	

E.J. Morrison Lt Col
O/C 87th FIELD AMBULANCE R.A.M.C.
29th DIVISION.

11/3/16

Programme of training for each evening Saturday 11th March 1916.

Day	7am–7.30am	9.30am–10.30am	11am–12noon	2.30pm–3.30pm
Monday	Physical Drill	Squad & Company Drill & Bayonet Drill	Route March	Lecture
Tuesday	Do	Do	A.D.M.S. Inspection Phlebotomists	Do
Wednesday	Do	Do		Do
Thursday	Do	Do	Squad & Company Drill & Stretcher Drill	Do
Friday	Do	Do	Do	Do
Saturday	Do	Do	Do	Do

Sgd.
Major Daw
Commanding 89th Field Ambulance

In Camp
11-3-16

A.D.M.S.
No. 21/22
Date 11.3.16
29TH DIVISION

83

① Appendix 10

Headquarters,
29th Division

Programme of work for week ending 18th March herewith.

[signature] Captain
for
Brigadier General
Comdg. 88th Bde.

11-2-13.

Mr H Wassermann Regiment

State of work for week ending Saturday 18th March 1916

Monday 13/3/16 Tuesday 14/3/16 Wednesday 15/3/16 Thursday 16/3/16 Friday 17/3/16 Saturday 18/3/16
Route March Been tested Boy Yearning 62 Rate March Musketry Interior to country
at below 62 Rate March at
6 P.M.   Musketry
    Night Operation 4 P.M.

Signallers
Signalling class Same as Monday Same as Monday Same as Monday Same as Monday Same as Monday
under Sgt Long

Musketry Instruction
Parade 11 a 2 Coy Same as Monday Same as Monday Same as Monday Same as Monday Same as Monday

L. Kearns Major
O/C 1/W—— Regt

2/3rd Hampshire Regiment.

Programme of Work. Week Ending 18th March 1916.

Date	Time	Nature of Work	Place
Monday 13.3.16	7–11. A.M.	Route march combined with protection on the march.	N.W. of Camp.
Tuesday 14.3.16	6.45–7.45 am 9.–11. am. 7. p.m.	Battalion Drill. Musketry standard tests. Fire direction, verbal. Night operations, concentration & advance in advance guard.	Camp.
Wednesday 15.3.16	7–11. Am.	Escort to Convoy.	W. of Camp.
Thursday 16.3.16	7–11. a.m. 7 p.m.	Outposts by day. Outposts by night.	— do —
Friday 17.3.16	6.45–7.45. 9. am.	Battalion Drill. Musketry standard test.	Camp.
Saturday 18.3.16	6.45–7.45. 9.30–12 noon.	Ceremonial drill. Kit Inspection.	

Classes of Instruction enlisted: Lewis Gunner, Sites, Leniner, Grenadier, Sniper, Stretch Bearer, Signaller.

R.W. Spencer Smith, Major
Comdg 2/4th Hampshire Regt.

Suez Camp. 10.3.16.

Programme of work for week ending 18th March 1916.

Date	6.45 to 7.30 am	9am to 12 noon	2 to 3 pm	Place	Remarks
13-3-16	Physical Training	Guard duties, Mounting - Inspecting. Handling arms, saluting, turning out, turning in, relieving sentries &c	Musketry	Vicinity of Camp.	
14-3-16	Cry run	Close order drill Sub-Officers and N.C.O's to drill a company.	Commanding Officers Parade		
15-3-16			Bayonet Fighting	Vicinity of Camp	
16-3-16			Commanding Officers Parade		
17-3-16	Physical Training	Advancing by short rushes. Instruction in Fire Orders. Fire control & Fire discipline, indication and recognition of targets, covering fire etc.	Musketry	Vicinity of Camp	
18-3-16	Physical Training	Kit - rifle, ammunition, equipment & non ration inspection. 10am C.O's inspection of lines.			

Notes:- Lewis Gunners - Bombers - Signallers & Snipers will parade with their Coys. for early morning parade. They will be at the disposal of their own Officers/commanders of the day, for instructional purposes.

SUEZ
10-3-16.

[signature]
Captain
Adjutant 1st Bn Essex Regiment

Programme of Work. Week Ending 18th March 1916

Time	Sunday	Monday	Tuesday	Wednesday	Thursday	Friday	Saturday
7. 7.30		Physical Training. Breakfast 8 am Kit Parade 7.30	Breakfast 7.0 Kit Parade 6.30	As Monday	As Monday	As Monday	As Monday
9.30 to 12.30	9.30 Church Parade	Saluting Drill. Ribbon Coy. Notebook Rifle Exercises Specialists Lewis M.G. Class Bombing Class	Coy Officers Route March 8. am Lewis Gun Class Bombing Class	Trench Dig & digging. Lewis G. Class Bombing Class	Guard & Sentries Lewis Gun Class Bombing Class	C.O.s Route March.	Kit Inspection by C.O at 9.30 am
2.0 to 3.0		Musketry. Signalling Class Bombing Class	As Monday	As Monday	As Monday	Pay	
3.0 to 4.0	5.30 Voluntary Church Parade	Officers Class NCO's Class	As Monday	As Monday	As Monday		

1st Royal Scots.
Sgt. 11.3.16.

J Bay[...]
Major
Commanding 5th Bn. Royal Scots.

Programme of Work — Newfoundland Regt

Time	Monday	Tuesday	Wednesday	Thursday	Friday	Saturday
7 a.m.	Physical	Physical	Physical	Physical	Physical	Physical
9 a.m.	Company Parades. Fire Control and extended order.	Battalion Parade Route March	Company Parades	Battalion Parade	Company Parades	Company Parades
2 p.m.	N.C.O.s Musketry Class	Lecture to Officers. Duties on board ship	Company Lecture Duties on board ship		Lecture by Platoon Commanders	Company Parades Musketry

Classes
 Lewis Gun
 Grenadier
 Snipers
 Stretcher bearer
 Signallers

A. L. Hadow
Lt Colonel
Comdg Newfoundland Regt.

95th Machine Gun Company

Programme of Work for Week ending Saturday 18th March 1916

	Sunday	Monday	Tuesday	Wednesday	Thursday	Friday	Saturday
9.45 – 8.15	Divine Service	Physical Training					
9.30 – 12		Section Training	Company Training	Section Training	Route March	Company Training	Kit & Equipment
2.15 – 3		Range Finders & Range Cards	Section	Rapid Firing		Service tie & Lecture	Inspection

Owen Coombe
10th March 1916

_____ Captain
Commanding 95th Machine Gun Company

29th DIVISION TACTICAL EXERCISE.

To illustrate – (i) Infantry attack over open ground.
(ii) Co-Operation of artillery and machine gun companies.

GENERAL IDEA.

Ref. attached sketch map.

An Eastern force retiring from Cairo to Suez, after a heavy reverse, is being followed up by a victorious Western Force.

SPECIAL IDEA. (WESTERN FORCE.)

On March 10th, the advanced guard of the Western Force regains touch with the rearguard of the Eastern Force, 4 miles N.W. of Suez.

Aeroplane reconnaissance reports that embarkation is in progress at Port Tewfik, and that Suez and the road leading to Port Tewfik is blocked with troops and artillery. The Eastern Force rearguard is covering Suez with about a Brigade, partly entrenched, at Bir Suez, with a post of about a Battalion half way between that and El Kubri, and another post of equal strength about a mile to the South of Bir Suez.

The advance guard (1 Division, less 1 Brigade) is ordered to attack Bir Suez, so that the main body shall not be delayed, when it arrives to attack Suez itself.

NOTES.

(1) Operation to commence at 4.p.m., by which hour, the troops will be in position, about 1 mile N.W. of Bir Suez, with scouts not closer than half a mile to the hostile position, which will be marked by blue flags.

(2) No ammunition will be carried, and all pouches will be carefully inspected prior to leaving Camp.

(3). Rapid bursts of artillery fire will be marked on the enemy's position artificially by smoke and dust, all orders to the artillery being repeated to the Directing Staff there by Helio.

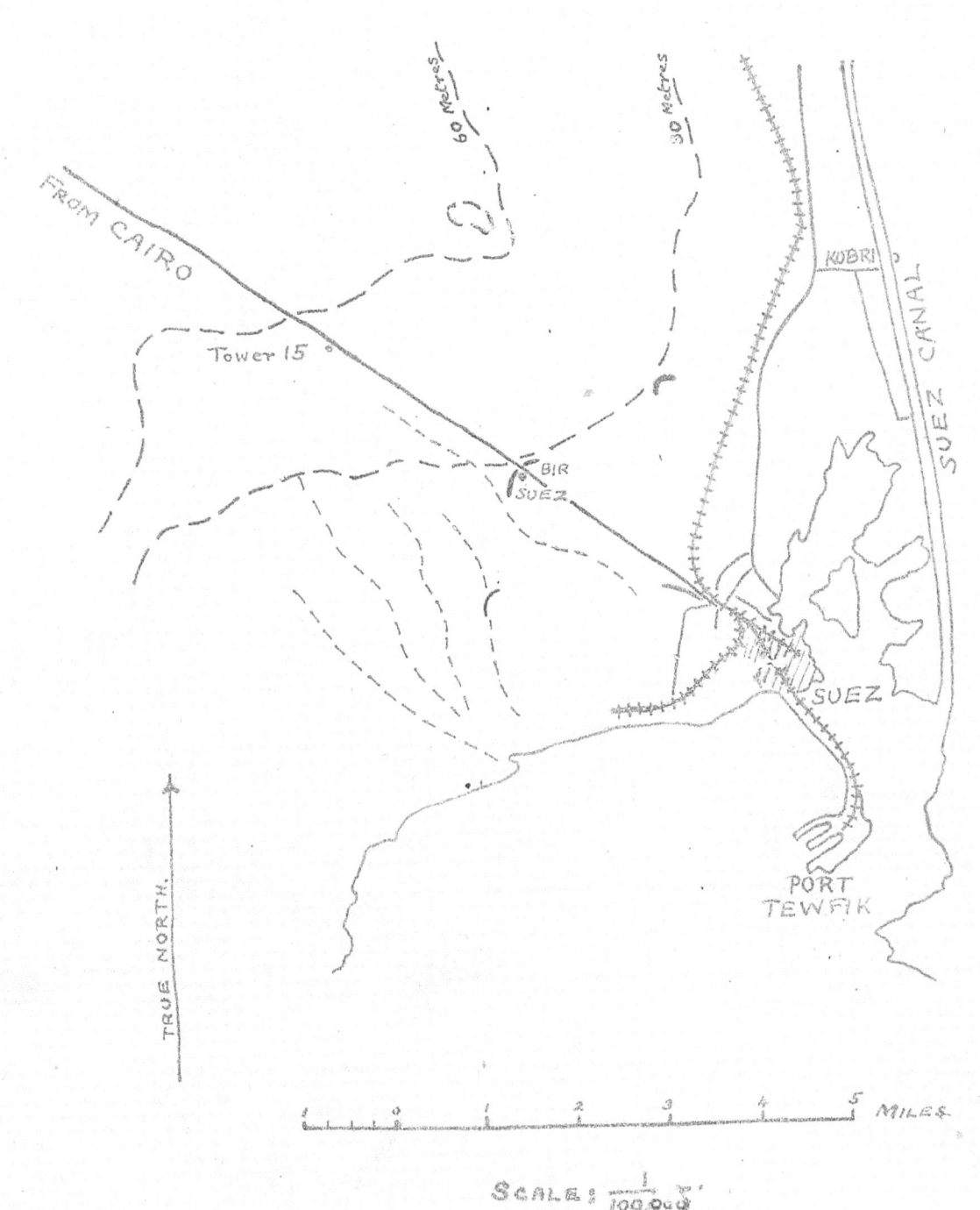

29th Divisional Order No.100.

1 mile West of
BIR SUEZ.
12/3/16.

1. Aeroplane reconnaissance reports that embarkation is in progress at Port Tewfik, and that Suez and the road leading to Port Tewfik is blocked with troops and artillery. Our advance guard reports that the enemy is covering Suez with about a Brigade, partly entrenched at BIR SUEZ, with a post of about a Battalion half way between that and EL KUBRI, and another post of equal strength about a mile to the South of BIR SUEZ.

2. The 86th Brigade will attack the position at BIR SUEZ, commencing at 1000 today, advancing on a front of about 800 yards with their left directed on the point where the telegraph wire passes BIR SUEZ. The advance will be covered by machine gun fire, and by bursts of artillery fire as detailed in para 6.

3. The Advance Guard will cover the left of this advance from hostile attack from the East of the telegraph line; one section of the 88th Brigade Machine Gun Company will be placed at the disposal of the O.C. Advance Guard (Lt.Col.Nelson, 1/R.Dublin Fus) for this purpose, and will report at the telegraph line one mile N.W. from BIR SUEZ.

4. The 88th Brigade will also detail two Companies and one section from their Machine Gun Company under to cover the right flank of the advance and to engage the hostile post South of BIR SUEZ.

5. The Divisional Artillery will detail one Brigade to engage the enemy post South of BIR SUEZ, and to cover the right flank of the attack.

6. The remainder of the Divisional Artillery will concentrate their fire on the position at BIR SUEZ, west of the telegraph line, and will fire in bursts of five minutes duration, commencing at 1000, and repeated every quarter of an hour.

7. The Cyclist Company will watch both flanks of the force, and will report direct to Divisional Headquarters.

8. The 88th Brigade will be in reserve, and will detail a Staff Officer to report at Divisional Headquarters at 0930.

9. Packs will be deposited in Brigade Dumps before the advance.
Casualties will remain on the field, and will not be evacuated till dusk.

10. Divisional Headquarters will be located in the Wadi one mile W. by S. of BIR SUEZ.

Issued at ....

Lieut.Colonel, G.S.
29th Division.

C.R.E.
C.R.A. (~~2 Copies~~)
86th & 88th Brigades.
Cyclists.

29th Division Order. (Special).

The following troops will assemble tomorrow at
8.30 p.m. under the command of Brig.General W. de L.Williams.
D.S.O. to take part in a tactical exercise:-

       1 Brigade. R.F.A.
       86th Brigade.
       88th Brigade.
       Divisional Cyclist Company.

2 Field Companies R.E. will mark the hostile position with flags and assist the Directing Staff to simulate the bursting of shells by means of smoke and dust.

2.   Dress - Marching Order without packs. No ammunition will be carried and all pouches will be carefully inspected prior to assembly.

3.   All communications will be carried out by visual signalling or orderlies.

4.   At the conclusion of the exercise, all officers down to Company Commanders will assemble when the officers' call sounds.

                                      Lieut.Colonel, G.S.

8th March 1916.   29th Division.

"A" Form.　　　　　　　　　　　　　　Army Form

MESSAGES AND SIGNALS.　　No. of Message

Prefix	Code	m.	Words	Charge			
Office of Origin and Service Instructions.					This message is on a/c of:	Recd. at ③	m.
			Sent			Date	
Priority			At	m.	Service.	From	
			To				
			By		(Signature of "Franking Officer.")	By	

TO { GOC Alexandria District
　　　9ᵗʰ Corps

Sender's Number	Day of Month	In reply to Number	
AB 497	11/3		AAA

Reference CR 15554/Q/7 from IGC I am relying on you to give necessary orders as regards remainder of 147ᵗʰ Brigade RFA and Artillery reinforcements. aaa addressed GOC Alexandria District repeated 9ᵗʰ Corps.

　　　　　　　　　　　　　　D.O.M. Capps

From　29ᵗʰ Div
Place
Time　0900

The above may be forwarded as now corrected.　(Z)

Censor.　Signature of Addressor or person authorised to telegraph in his name

* This line should be erased if not required.
8350　S. B. Ltd. Wt. W4843/541—50,000. 9/14. Forms C2121/10.

"C" Form (Duplicate).   Army Form C.2¹

MESSAGES AND SIGNALS.   No. of Message

	Charges to Pay.	Office Stamp.
	£ s. d.	YB / 11.III.16

Service Instructions.   Alexandria   1655

Handed in at 29th Div. Suez   Office   m. Received   m.

TO   GR 1248   11th ANZAC

Sender's Number   Day of Month   In reply to Number   AAA

Cannot trace artillery reinforcements in Alexandria

Ferial

FROM PLACE & TIME

Oppg. 11

1 — 4

Secret

Appendix II

29th Division.

2nd Flight - 29th Div

Attached berthing allotment for hired transport "Miltiades", which will embark at Suez on 13th March.

Units to be embarked are :-

	Officers	O.R.	
Div. H.Q.	10	65	
" R.A. H.Q.	6	18	} 1 p.m.
(illegible)		150	
1/W.Riding Fld.Co	7	155	
87th F.Amb.	9	244	
1st Lancs. Fus.	33	704	12 noon
80th Bde. M.G.	4	29	} 1 p.m.
	67	1205	

Band.   30 - 1 p.m.

The embarkation orders previously issued will apply, maximum accommodation, 88 officers, 1280 other ranks.

These orders are issued from this office as letter from E.O.C., Cairo has gone astray.

Meacham
Lieutenant-Colonel,
for D.A. & Q.M.G.
9th Army Corps.

12-3-16.

Copies to :-
29th Division.
Base Commandant.
E.T.O.
N.T.O.

No 2 Berth on North Wall ready at 8 A.M.
Baggage after 9 A.M.

1/Leaves Fusm.

Tax 9/-

Ships agitus
R.S.M.
C.Q.M.S.   to report £ 10 a.m
8 O.Rks   at Embarkatn Office

Brig. Embarkatn Station of arrival
rolls of sailings

18-3-20.

DAQMG
86th & ~~88th~~ Brigades.
C.R.A.
A.D.M.S.
Camp Commandant.
O.C.Cyclists.
1st West Riding Field Co.
A.D.V.S.
LT. WHITTAM. LANCS FUS. (Ship's adjt.).
D.A.Q.M.G.

Orders have been received for the following troops to embark on H.T. "Miltiades" at Suez on 13th March: the ship will be berthed at No.2 Berth on North Wall.

Divisional Headquarters.	5 Officers.	97	Other Ranks.
R.A.Headquarters.	6 "	20	" "
1st W.Riding Field Co.	7 "	180	" "
87th Field Ambulance.	9 "	247	" "
1st Lancs. Fusiliers.	25 "	704	" "
86th Brigade H.Q.	4 "	52	" "
Band.		30	" "
	57 "	1280	" "

Any alterations in the above figures will be notified to 29th Divisional Headquarters by wire immediately.

2. Maximum accommodation is 59 Officers, 1280 Other Ranks.

3. Officers will be provided with lunch on board ship, the first meal for troops will be tea at 4 p.m., they should therefore have dinners before they march off.

4. Baggage must be at the Docks at 9 a.m. Units will arrange direct with O.C.Train for necessary transport.

5. The Lancs.Fusiliers will be at the Docks ready to embark at 12 noon and the remainder of the troops at 1 p.m. tomorrow.

6. Embarkation states and nominal rolls both in duplicate will be handed in by 8.p.m. tonight to the O.C. Lancs.Fus. Suez Camp.

D. M? Cay?
Lieut.Colonel, G.S.
29th Division.

12th March 1915.

The Ship's adjt. S.M. Q.M.S. and S.O.R. will report at 10 am at Embarkation office at Suez Docks with nominal rolls and Embarkation states both in duplicate

"C" Form (Duplicate).
MESSAGES AND SIGNALS.
Army Form C. 2123.

No. of Message..........

Qm tt   90   CP
                 pg

Charges to Pay. Office Stamp.
£   s.   d.
                   ARMY
                   YB1 12.III.15.

Service Instructions.

Handed in at ......9.00...... Office ...8.9.... m. Received ......m.

TO
          29th Div Suez Camp

Sender's Number Day of Month In reply to Number
                      12   AAA

Reference embarkation militades thirteenth
aaa Confirming telephone message
Lancs Fusrs will embark 12 noon
remaining troops one pm aaa
Baggage to be down as
soon after nine am as
possible aaa Ships adjutant ships
sergt major and ships qms
with eight other ranks to
report embarkation office 10 am
bringing in duplicate embarkation
states and nominal rolls for
all troops embarking aaa Officers
will be served with lunch
but troops first meal 4 pm
aaa ship will be alongside
north wall number two berth

FROM
PLACE & TIME   Embarking Suez

(25555). M.R.Co.,Ltd. Wt.W1789/1402. 70,000 Pads—6/15. Forms/C.2123.

SECRET

C.R.15584/Q/8.

The General Officer Commanding,
    9th Corps,
        Suez.

Second Flight - 29th Division

1.   Attached please find Berthing Allotment for the Hired Transport MILTIADES which will embark at Suez on 13th March.

2.   Units to be embarked are:-

        Divn. Hdqrs.
        Divn. Artillery Hdqrs.
        G.G.Cable Section.
        1st West Riding Field Coy.
        87th Field Ambulance.
        1st Lancashire Fusiliers.
        86th Infty. Bde. Hdqrs.

3.   The embarkation orders previously issued will apply.

Cairo,
                                          Bt.Lt.Colonel,
11th March, 1916.   for Inspector General of Communications.

Copies to:- D.Q.M.G.,G.H.Q.
            D.A.G.3rd Ech.
            G.O.C.29th Divn.
            Base Cdt. Suez.
             "   " Port Said.
            Admt.Cdt.Ismailia.
            P.N.T.O.
            N.T.O.Port Said.
             "   Suez.
            E.S.O.Port Said.
             "   Suez.
            H.of B. F.E.
            D.of S. L.B.

MOVE OF 2nd. FLIGHT, 29th. Division.
13th. March.
ALLOTMENT OF BERTHING ACCOMMODATION

Suez, 13th. March.
H. T. MILTIADES.

	Officers	Other ranks.
Maximum Accommodation	88	1250
Divisional Headquarters	10	63
Divisional Artillery Headquarters	6	13
G. G. Cable Section	1	35
1st. West Riding Field Company	7	160
87th. Field Ambulance	8	246
1st. Lancashire Fusiliers	31	704
86th. Infantry Brigade Hdqrs.	4	32
	67	1253

d

"A" Form. Army Form C. 2121.
MESSAGES AND SIGNALS. No. of Message

TO A.D.R. GHQ.

Sender's Number.	Day of Month	In reply to Number	AAA
GA 245	3/3		

Number of draught horses required to complete Divisional Artillery at SUEZ is 90 aaa D.Q.M.G. GHQ and 9th Corps informed. Officers chargers required to complete establishment other than Artillery 189 aaa D.Q.M.G. GHQ and 9th Corps informed.

From 74th Div.

"A" Form. Army Form C. 2121.

MESSAGES AND SIGNALS.

Priority

TO: AQMG Cairo 9th Corps.   ADR Cairo

Sender's Number: AB 499. Day of Month: 11/3.   AAA

Reference my GA 245 of 3rd inst addressed ADR GHQ stating that 189 officers chargers were required to complete establishment other than Artillery can you please inform me where these horses will be sent to embark or if they will be sent to Suez aaa In accordance with para 3 of CR 15554/Q/6 from IGC we are keeping back sufficient personnel to look after these 189 chargers when they are received aaa addressed AQMG Cairo repeated ADR GHQ 9th Corps.

D O'Ky Capt

From: 29th Div
Time: 1705

"A" Form.
Army Form C. 2121.

MESSAGES AND SIGNALS.

No. of Message _____

Prefix ____ Code ____ m.	Words	Charge	This message is on a/c of:	Recd. at ____ m.
Office of Origin and Service Instructions.	Sent			Date ____
Priority	At ____ m.		Service.	From ____
DO	To ____			By ____
	By ____		(Signature of "Franking Officer.")	

TO { A.D.R. G.H.Q.

Sender's Number	Day of Month	In reply to Number	
A.B 500	11/3		A A A

Please provide the 189 chargers asked for in my GA 245 of 3rd inst and inform Daglock to complete establishment and inform Daglock when you can provide them aaa also please inform me aaa the necessary personnel to look after these horses is being left behind here and will be sent to the port of embarkation as soon as Daglock can inform me where to send them aaa Please wire early aaa addressed ADR GHQ repeated Daglock AAMG Cairo, 9th Corps.

D. M. [signature]

From 29th Div
Place ____
Time 2200

The above may be forwarded as now corrected. (Z)

Censor. Signature of Addressor or person authorized to telegraph in his name

* This line should be erased if not required.

"A" Form.　　　　　　　　　　　　　　　　Army Form C. 2121.

MESSAGES AND SIGNALS.　　No. of Message _____

Prefix ___ Code ___ m.	Words	Charge	This message is on a/c of:	Recd. at ___ m.
Office of Origin and Service Instructions.				Date ___
	Sent At ___ m.		___ Service.	From ___
Priority D₀	To ___			
	By ___		(Signature of "Franking Officer.")	By ___

TO { Daglock   A.D.R. G.H.Q.
     9ᵗʰ Corps. A.Q.M.G. Cairo.

| Sender's Number | Day of Month | In reply to Number | AAA |
| AB501 | 11/3 | 4521 | |

A.D.R. G.H.Q. has been asked to provide the
189 chargers already indented for in my
GA 245 addressed to him on 3ʳᵈ inst and repeated
to in my AB499 to A.Q.M.G. Cairo today aaa
Can you please provide accommodation for
them if so please wire where and when
they will be embarked aaa I am keeping
the necessary personnel here till I hear
from you when I will send them direct
to the port you select for embarkation you have sabot
aaa addressed The 189 chargers are shown in
my marching out state of today aaa address
Daglock repeated A.D.R. G.H.Q. 9ᵗʰ Corps.
A.Q.M.G. Cairo

D. M??Capp

From 29ᶜ Div.
Place
Time 2/53

The above may be forwarded as now corrected.　(Z)

　　　　　　　　　　Censor.　Signature of Addresser or person authorised to telegraph in his name

* This line should be erased if not required.

8350 S. B. Ltd. Wt. W4843/541—50,000. 9/14. Forms C2121/10.

"C" Form (Duplicate).   Army Form C. 2123.
MESSAGES AND SIGNALS.
No. of Message

Charges to Pay. £ s. d.

Office Stamp. YB1 12.III.16

Service Instructions. 1 of 2 addresses

Handed in at GHQ   Office 0005 m. Received 0005 m.

TO   29th Divn

Sender's Number	Day of Month	In reply to Number	AAA
NR1044	12th		

29th Divn wires please provide the 184 Chargers asked for in my GA 245 of 3rd Inst to complete Establishment and inform Daglock when you can provide them AAA Also please inform me AAA The necessary personnel to look after these horses is being left behind here and will be sent to the port of embarkation as soon as daglock can inform me where to send them AAA Please wire early aaa addressed ADR GHQ reptd Daglock army Cairo 9th Corps AAA
(Ends)

FROM
PLACE & TIME

"C" Form (Duplicate).   Army Form C. 2123.
MESSAGES AND SIGNALS.

No. of Message

Charges to Pay — £ s. d.   Office Stamp. 12.III.16 TELEGRAPHS

Service Instructions.

Handed in at .... Office .... m. Received 0053 m.

TO   (2) 29th Divn

Sender's Number	Day of Month	In reply to Number	AAA
ends by inst 9th	The my repeated Corps	chargers VR O's Daylock	were demanded of 3rd 29th Divn

FROM PLACE & TIME   ADR GHQ

"C" Form (Original).   Army Form C. 2123.

MESSAGES AND SIGNALS.

Prefix	Code	Words 63	Received From Grayob	Sent, or sent out At ___ m. To ___ By ___	Office Stamp YB1 11.III.16 TELEGRAPHS
Charges to collect £ s. d.					
Service Instructions.					

Handed in at Cairo By   Office 2039 m. Received 2131 m.

TO   29th Divn Ismailia

*Sender's Number 4521	Day of Month 11th	In reply to Number A/B/499	AAA

Nothing is known of any charges beyond those shown in your state aaa no remounts has been provided or contemplated for any animals not shown in your state aaa personnel referred to should not be detained except as ordered aaa addressed 29th Div repeated A D & R G H Q 9th Corps

FROM PLACE & TIME   Haglock Cairo

*This line should be erased if not required
(25555). M.R.Co.,Ltd. Wt.W1789/1402. 70,000 Pads—6/15. Forms/C.2123.

"A" Form.
MESSAGES AND SIGNALS.
Army Form C. 2121.

Prefix	Code	m.	Words	Charge			No. of Message	
Office of Origin and Service Instructions.					This message is on a/c of :		Recd. at	m.
Priority DO			Sent				Date	
			At	m.		Service.	From	
			To					
			By		(Signature of "Franking Officer.")		By	

TO { A.Q.M.G. Cairo. A.D.R. G.H.Q.
     9th Corps. Dagloch.

Sender's Number: AB 504   Day of Month: 12/3   In reply to Number: AAA

Reference my AB 501 of yesterday aaa I have been told by ADR GHQ by telephone that the 189 horses are being embarked at Alexandria today aaa Please wire whether you wish me to send personnel from here to take charge of these horses aaa ADR could not tell me which ship they are being embarked on aaa address AQMG Cairo repeated Dagloch, 9th Corps ADR GHQ

D. Oly Copps

From: 74th Div.
Place:
Time: 1230.

The above may be forwarded as now corrected. (Z)

Censor. Signature of Addressor or person authorized to telegraph in his name
* This line should be erased if not required.
8350 S.B. Ltd. Wt. W4843/541-50,000. 9/14. Forms C2121/10.

(COPY)

D.M.S., M.E.F. 1460/108,
dated 10/3/16.

D.D.M.S.,

    9th. Corps.

One Sanitary Section is being posted to Suez. As Divisions leaving the force are to take Sanitary Sections with them, the Sanitary Section now being posted will replace the one leaving.

G.H.Q.,
10/3/16.

(Sd) W.G.A. BEDFORD,
Surgeon-General, D.M.S., M.E.F.

(2)

D.A. & Q.M.G.,

    9th. Corps.

The Sanitary Section to leave with the 29th. Division is Number 16, situated adjacent to 17th. Stationary Hospital, Tewfik.

H.Q., 9th. Corps.
12/3/16.

Colonel, A.M.S.,
D.D.M.S., 9th. Corps.

URGENT

29th Division.

      For information and necessary action.

      Daglock should be informed by wire of embarkation strength of this unit.

12/3/16   Lieut. Colonel.
                        for D.A.&.Q.M.G. 9th Corps.

"A" Form.
Army Form C. 2121.

MESSAGES AND SIGNALS.

Prefix	Code	m.	Words	Charge	This message is on a/c of	Recd. at	m.
Office of Origin and Service Instructions.			Sent			Date	
			At	m.	Service.	From	
			To				
			By		(Signature of "Franking Officer.")	By	

TO ADMS

| Sender's Number. | Day of Month | In reply to Number | |
| G 664 | 12 | | AAA |

Instructions received that Number 16 Sanitary Section detailed depart to 17 Stationary Hospital TENFIK will proceed with Division as per [illegible] as instructions letter sent by [illegible].

From R.J. Dunn
Place
Time 1130

appx 12

(1-3)

Appendix 12

C.R.15584/Q/9

SECRET.

General Officer Commanding,
    9th Corps, Suez.

THIRD FLIGHT 29th DIVISION.

1.   Attached please find berthing allotment for the Hired Transport "TRANSYLVANIA" which will embark at Alexandria on the 15th March.

2.   Units to be embarked are:-
        88th Brigade Machine Gun Company
        88th Infantry Brigade Head Quarters.
        4th Worcester Regiment.
        2nd Hants Regiment.
        1st Essex Regiment.

3.   Train timings and train allotments are attached.

4.   The orders previously issued will apply.

                                    J.M. Broadbent
                                    Bt.Lieut-Colonel,
Cairo.
12th March 1916.   for Inspector General of Communications.

Copies to D.Q.M.G., G.H.Q.
          D.A.G. 3rd Echelon.
          G.O.C. 29th Division.
          G.O.C. Alexandria District.
          Base Commdt. Alexandria.
          Base Commdt. Suez.
          P.N.T.O.
          D.N.T.O. Alexandria.
          E.S.O. Alexandria.
          D.R.T.
          A.D.R.T. Ismailia.
          D.A.D.R.T. Cairo, Alex. Ismailia. Suez.
          R.T.O. Suez.
          H. of B. Force in Egypt.
          D. of S. Levant Base.

3rd Flight 29th Division.
C.R.15584/Q/9.
Table No. 8.

ALLOTMENT OF BERTHING ACCOMMODATION.

Alexandria, 15th March, 1916.

UNIT	TRANSYLVANIA	
	Officers.	Other Ranks.
Maximum accommodation.	523	2493.
Machine Gun Co. 88th Bde.	8 ~~9~~	~~138~~ 137
88th Infantry Bde. Hqrs.	2	~~33~~ 51
4th Worcesters.	30	~~814~~ 808
2nd Hants.	27	~~924~~ 909
1st Essex.	~~28~~ 33	~~1009~~ 997
Chaplain.	1	-
TOTAL	~~96~~ 102	2918 2902

3014

411

M.P.

C.R.15584/O/9.
Train Timing No.4.

TRAIN TIMINGS FOR THE MOVE OF 3RD FLIGHT, 29TH DIVISION ON 14/15TH MARCH.

No. of Train.	Type.	Loading Station.	Time ready for loading.	Time leave loading Station.	Destination.	Arrive.
834/701.	Infantry.	SUEZ CAMP.	5.30.p.m.	7.30.p.m.	GABBARY DOCK.	5.40.a.m.
840/707.	Infantry.	SUEZ CAMP.	8.20.p.m.	10.20.p.m.	TRANSYLVANIA.	8.45.a.m.
802/711.A.	Infantry.	SUEZ CAMP.	11.10.p.m.	1.10.a.m.	TRANSYLVANIA.	11.15.a.m.
808/717.A.	Infantry.	SUEZ CAMP.	2.a.m.	4.10.a.m.	TRANSYLVANIA.	2.30.p.m.
814/727.A.	Infantry.	SUEZ CAMP.	5.a.m.	8.a.m.	TRANSYLVANIA.	6.25.p.m.

FOR TRAIN ALLOTMENTS SEE TRAIN ALLOTMENTS NO.4.

M.P.

3RD FLIGHT 29TH DIVISION.

C.R.15584/Q/9.
Train Allotments No.4.

29TH DIVISION, SUEZ CAMP TO ALEXANDRIA TO EMBARK ON TRANSYLVANIA.

1st Train, Infantry, No.834/701.

Unit.	Officers.	Other Ranks.
1st Essex Regiment.	20 ~~35~~ 22	~~585~~ ~~90~~ 585

2nd Train, Infantry, No.840/707.

1st Essex Regiment.	~~8~~ 11	~~424~~ 412
88th Brigade, Machine Gun Co.	~~8~~ 9	~~138~~ 137
88th Brigade Headquarters.	2	~~33~~ 51
Chaplain.	1	—
	~~19~~ 23	~~595~~ 600

3rd Train, Infantry, No.802/711.A.

4th Worcesters.	20	~~585~~ 579

4th Train, Infantry, No.808/717.A.

4th Worcesters.	10	229
2nd Hants.	10	~~350~~ 340
	20	~~579~~ 569

5th Train, Infantry, No.814/727.A.

2nd Hants.	17	~~574~~ 569.

FOR TRAIN TIMINGS SEE TRAIN TIMINGS NO.4.

M.P.

Headqrs 88th Brigade
O.C. Train.
R.T.O. Sidi Camp.

1. Orders have been received for the following troops to embark on the H.T. TRANSYLVANIA at Alexandria on 15th March.

~~Headqrs 88th Brigade~~

88th Brigade M Gun Coy.
88th Infy Brigade Headqrs
4th Worcester Regt.
2nd Hants Regt.
1st Essex Regt.

2. Bething allotments, train timings and train allotments are attached.

3. Units will arrange direct with O C Train for necessary transport.

4. Rations for the 15th March should be taken in addition to the Reserve Ration.

5. Nominal rolls and embarkation forms will be made out in quadruplicate and handed to the Senior Officer of each train who will hand them to the Embarkation Officer at Alexandria.

S.D.M.
Captain G.S.
29th Division

13/3/16.

M.C.R. 15584/Q9
Lille to 8

ALLOTMENT OF BERTHING ACCOMMODATION.

Alexandria 15th March 1916.

UNIT.	TRANSYLVANIA	
Maximum Accommodation	OFFICERS 523	OTHER RANKS 2493.
Machine Gun Coy. 88th Bde.	9	137
88th Infantry Bde. Hqrs	2	51
4th Worcesters	30	808
2nd Hants.	27	909
1/Essex.	33	997
Chaplain	1	
TOTAL.	102	2902

Note. The following are the final figures to entrain

88th B. M.G Coy	9	137
" H.Q"	3	57
4" Worcester	29	796
2nd Hants	27	913
1/ Essex.	32	1000
Chaplain	1	
	101	2903

S.O.

TRAIN TIMINGS FOR THE MOVE OF 2nd FLIGHT 24th DIVISION
ON 14.15 th MARCH

No OF TRAIN	TYPE	LOADING STATION	TIME READY FOR LOADING	TIME LEAVE LOADING STATION	DESTINATION	ARRIVE
834/707	Infantry	Auly Camp	5.30 pm	7.30 pm	(GARDABY ROCK) TRANSYLVANIA	5.40 am
846/707	Infantry	Auly Camp	8.20 am	10.20 pm	TRANSYLVANIA	8.45 am
502/111 A	Infantry	Auly Camp	11.0 pm	1.00 am	TRANSYLVANIA	11.05 am
503/111 A	Infantry	Auly Camp	2 am	4.10 am	TRANSYLVANIA	2.10 pm
614/727 A	Infantry	Auly Camp	5 am	6 am	TRANSYLVANIA	6.25 pm

FOR TRAIN ALLOTMENTS SEE TRAIN ALLOTMENTS No 6.

3RD FLIGHT 29TH DIVISION.

G.R. 15574/Q/9.
Train Allotment No: 4.

29TH DIVISION, SUEZ CAMP to ALEXANDRIA to embark on TRANSYLVANIA.

1st Train Infantry No. 834/701.

UNIT.	OFFICERS	OTHER RANKS.
1st Essex Regt.	22	585.

2nd Train Infantry No. 840/707.

1st Essex Regt.	11	412.
88th Bde. Mach. Gun. Coy.	9	137.
88th Bde Headquarters	2	51
Chaplain.	1	.
	23	600

3rd Train Infantry No. 802/711A.

4th Worcesters.	20	579.

4th Train Infantry No. 805/717A

4th Worcesters	10	229.
2nd Hants	10	340.
	20	569.

5th Train Infantry No. 814/727A.

2nd Hants.	17	569.

FOR TRAIN TIMINGS SEE TRAIN TIMINGS No. 4.

SECRET.

Wire has been received from Daglock, Cairo, as follows :-

"Reference my 15584/Q/10. Hired transport "Alaunia" now reported by Naval transport capable of carrying more troops 1/5 Royal Scots will proceed by this ship instead of "Lake Manitoba".

16th Sanitary Section also to embark if accommodation available.

Orders by first signal bag tomorrow.

Inform Embarking and N.T.O."

================

29th Division.

For information and necessary action.

13/3/16.

Needham
Lieut Colonel.
D.A.&Q.M.G. 9th Corps.

appx 13

(1 - 6)

2nd. & 3rd. FLIGHTS, 29th. DIVISION.   C.R.15584/Q/10.

Appendix 13

The
    General Officer Commanding
        9th. CORPS.

----

1.   Attached please find Berthing Allotments for H.T. ALAUNIA (2nd. Flight) and H.T. LAKE MANITOBA (3rd. Flight) which will embark at SUEZ. *on 14th and 15th inst respectively*

(Dates will be notified later.)

2.   The units to be embarked are :

    Second Flight.

        2nd. Royal Fusiliers
        1st. Royal Munster Fusiliers
        Chaplain
        West Kent Field Company
        Newfoundland Battalion.
        1/5 Royal Scots

    Third Flight *16th Sanitary Section (if accommodation available)*

        Machine Gun Company 86th. Brigade.
        89th. Field Ambulance
        1/5th. Royal Scots
        Divisional Ammunition Column Personnel.
        Cyclist Company.
        Records Section
        16th Sanitary Section.

3.   The embarkation orders issued previously will apply.

4.   The 29th. Divisional Records Section will join the Lake Manitoba at PORT SAID. Date to be notified later.

5.   This completes the allotments to transports of the 29th. Division, with the exception of the Base Depot.

                                    P.H. Broadbent

Cairo,   Bt. Lt. Colonel,
12th. March, 1916.   For Inspector General of Communications.

    Copies to ---
        D.Q.M.G. G.H.Q.   E.S.O. ALEX.
        D.A.G. 3rd. Ech.   D.R.T.
        G.O.C. 29th. Div.   A.D.R.T. ISMAILIA.
        G.O.C. ALEX.   D.A.D.R.T. CAIRO, ALEX.
        Base Cdt., ALEX.   ISMAILIA & SUEZ.
        BASE Cdt. SUEZ.   R.T.O. SUEZ.
        P.N.T.O.   H. of B. F.E.
        D.N.T.O. ALEX.   D. of S. L.B.

C.R 15584/O/10.
Table No 9.

2nd. FLIGHT, 29th.DIVISION.

ALLOTMENT OF BERTHING ACCOMMODATION.

Suez.

H.T. ALAUNIA

Unit	Officers	Other Ranks
Maximum Accommodation.	200	1800
2nd. Royal Fusiliers	29	906
1st.Royal Munster Fusiliers	24	290
Chaplain	1	-
West Kent Field Company	5	153
Newfoundland Battalion	25	577
R. Scott	26	308
	~~84~~ 110	1926- ~~22~~

d

C.R. 15585/G/10.
Table 10.

THIRD FLIGHT, 29th DIVISION.

ALLOTMENT OF BERTHING ACCOMMODATION.

SUEZ.

H.T. LAKE MANITOBA

Unit	Officers	Other Ranks
Maximum Accommodation	104	974
16th Sanitary Section	1	37
Machine Gun Company, 86 Brigade	9	106
89th. Field Ambulance	10	226
~~1/5th. Royal Scots~~	~~26~~	~~306~~
Divisional Ammunition Column Personnel	1	35 (to join at P.Said).
Cyclists Company	~~19~~ 2	~~215~~ 191.
Records Section	2	32 (to join at P.Said).
Signal Coy.	2	35
	67	920

Div Staff.

Balc 37 54 94
         29 35 65

Sanitary
Signals

d

The following telephone message has been received from A.Q.M.G. Cairo this morning.

"Reference my 15584/Q/10. The hired transport "Alaunia" will embark at Suez to-morrow, 14th instant.

Hired transport "Lake Manitoba" will embark at Suez on Wednesday 15th instant".

29th Division.

For information and necessary action.

13/3/16.

Lieut. Colonel.
for D.A.&.Q.M.G.
9th Army Corps.

C.R.15584/Q/11.

General Officer Commanding,
9th Corps Suez.

----

1.   With reference to my C.R.15584/Q/10 of the 12th instant, the Hired Transport "ALAUNIA", on arrival has been found capable of carrying:-

   120 Officers   2224 Other Ranks instead of the maximum numbers previously shown.

2.   The 1/5th Battalion Royal Scots, previously allotted to the Hired Transport "LAKE MANITOBA" will accordingly be allotted to the Hired Transport "ALAUNIA".

3.   The General Officer Commanding, 29th Division, telegraphs the strength of No.16 Sanitary Section as 1 officer, and 37 other ranks. This Unit which does not appear in the states rendered, will embark in the Hired Transport "ALAUNIA" if accomodation is available. If otherwise it will embark in the Hired Transport "LAKE MANITOBA".

F.M. Broadbent
Bt.Lieut-Colonel.

Cairo.

13th March 1916.   for Inspector General of Communications.

Copies to   D.Q.M.G.,G.H.Q.   E.S.O.Alexandria.
            D.A.G.3rd Echelon.   D.R.T.
            G.O.C.29th Divn.   A.D.R.T.Ismailia.
            G.O.C.Alexandria.   D.A.D.R.T.Cairo.Alex.
            Base Commdt.Alex.   Ismailia and Suez.
            Base Commdt.Suez.   R.T.O.Suez.
            P.N.T.O.   H.of B. Force in Egypt.
            D.N.T.O.Alexandria.   D.of S. Levant Base.

C.R. L5584/Q/12.

The
    General Officer Commanding
        9th. Corps, SUEZ.

In confirmation of my telephone message this morning please note that the H.T. ALAUNIA will embark at SUEZ on the 14th. March, and the LAKE MANITOBA on the 16th.

                                                P. N. Broadbent
                                                Bt. Lt. Colonel,

Cairo,   For Inspector General of
13th. March, 1916.   Communications.

Copies to ---
    D.Q.M.G. G.H.Q.   E.S.C. ALEX.
    D.A.G. 3rd. Ech.   D.R.T.
    G.O.C. 29th. Div.   A.D.R.T. ISMAILIA.
    G.O.C. ALEX.   D.A.D.R.T. CAIRO. ALEX.
    Base Cdt., ALEX.   ISMAILIE & SUEZ.
    Base Cdt. SUEZ.   R.T.O. SUEZ.
    P.N.T.C.   H. of B. F.E.
    D.N.T.O. ALEX.   D. of S. L.B.

                                                           d

To Headqrs. 9th Bde.
" OC 2/Royal Fus.
     1/R Munster Fus.
     W. Kent Field Coy R.E.
     ~~16th Sanitary Section.~~ [x'd out]
     OC Train.

1. Orders have been received for the following troops to embark on H.T. Alaunia (2nd Flight) at Suez on the 14th March:-

   Second Flight.
     2nd Royal Fusiliers
     1st Royal Munster Fus.
     Chaplain
     West Kent Field Coy
     Newfoundland Battalion
     1/5th B. Scots
     ~~16th Sanitary Section~~ (if accommodation available).

2. Allotments of berthing accommodation are attached.

3. Duplicate nominal rolls and embarkation returns will be handed to the OC NFLD Regt. by 0730 tomorrow.

4. The OC NFLD Regt. will detail a Ship's Adjutant, Ship's Sgt. Qmaster Sergt, and 8 other ranks all of whom will report at the Embarkation office Suez Docks at 0930 tomorrow with the nominal rolls and embarkation returns mentioned above.

5. Troops will be at Suez Docks at the following hours:-
     2/R. Fusiliers at 1100.
     W. Kent Field Coy. 1130.
     1/Royal Mun. Fus. 1200.
     Newfoundland Regt. 1245
     1/5th B.Scots. 1330.
     ~~16th Sanitary Sect. 1400.~~

6. ~~Troopers will~~ Lunch will be provided for officers at 1300 on board ship. Tea will be the first meal for the troops, at 1600. The troops should therefore have their dinners before marching off.

7. Units will arrange direct with OC Train for necessary transport. Baggage must be at Suez Docks by 0900.

D. M.
Capt. S.
29th Division

13/3/16.

2nd Flight 29th Division

CR 15584/9/10.
Table No: 9.

ALLOTMENT OF BERTHING ACCOMMODATION —

Suez.
H.T. ALAUNIA

UNIT	OFFICERS	OTHER RANKS
MAXIMUM ACCOMMODATION	200.	1800.
2nd Royal Fusiliers	29	906.
1st R. Munster Fus.	24	290.
Chaplain	1	—
West Kent Field Coy.	5	153.
Newfoundland Battn.	25	577.
1st R. Scots	26	301.
~~H.Q. Sanitary Section~~	~~*~~	~~37~~
	110	2227

Office Copy.   Secd   ⑤

To O.C.
16th Sanitary Section,
86th Bde. M.Gun. Coy.
89th Field Ambulance
Cyclists
Signals
Train.

1. Orders have been received for the following troops to embark on the H.T. MANITOBA on the 15th or 16th March (probably the latter) at Suez:–
    86th Bde M.Gun. Coy.
    89th Field Amb.
    Div. Ammunition Column Personnel.
    Cyclist Coy.
    Records Section.
    16th Sanitary Section.
    Signal Coy attachments.
Further orders will follow as to exact date and times of embarkation.

2. Units will prepare nominal rolls and Embarkation Returns, both in duplicate, and will hand them over to Capt Beckwith at a time to be notified later.

3. Capt. Beckwith, Commdg 86th Bde. M.Gun. Coy, will be O.C. troops on board. He will select a Ship's Adjutant, Sergt. Major, Orderly Sgt. and 6 other ranks, all of whom will be at the Embarkation Office, Suez Docks, at a time to be notified later, and will there hand in the nominal rolls and embarkation returns mentioned above.

4. Allotments of berthing / accommodation are attached.

5. Units will arrange direct with the O.C. Train for necessary transport.

6. Tea at 1600 will probably be the first meal for troops on board; they should therefore arrange to have dinner before marching off. Lunch will probably be served to officers at 1300 on board. Further notification will be given with regard to meals as soon as it is definitely settled.

             DT Mey
             Capt. GS
             29th Division.

NOTE to 16th Sany Sect → 13/3/16.
Ref para 2, the nominal rolls and embarkation returns of the 16th Sany Section may be handed in to the Ship's Adjutant at Embarkation Office Suez Docks at a time to be notified later.
             (sdd) DO.

G.R. 15586/Q/10.
Table 10.

Third Flight 29th Division

ALLOTMENT OF BERTHING ACCOMMODATION -

Suez
H.T. LAKE MANITOBA.

Unit.	Officers	Other Ranks.
MAXIMUM ACCOMMODATION.	104	974.
1st. Sanitary Section.	1	37.
Machine gun Coy. 86th Bde.	9	106.
89th Field Ambulance.	10	226.
Div'l Ammunition Column Personnel.	1	35 (1 join at P. Said.)
Cyclists Company.	2	191.
Records Section.	2	32 (1 join at P. Said)
Signal Coy.	2	35.
29th Div. Staff	2	3.
	29	665

"A" Form.   Army Form
MESSAGES AND SIGNALS.   No. of Message

Prefix	Code	m.	Words	Charge	This message is on a/c of:	Recd. at	m.
Office of Origin and Service Instructions.			Sent			Date	
			At	m.	Service.	From	
			To				
			By		(Signature of "Franking Officer.")	By	

TO { 86 Bde M. Gun Coy / OC 86th Sanitary Section
     89 Fd Ambulance
     86 Cyclist
     86 Signals }

Sender's Number	Day of Month	In reply to Number	AAA
AB 534	4/3		

Reference orders issued yesterday aaa Embarkation will take place Sunday morning of 16th inst as follows aaa Baggage to be at Suez Docks by 0900 with suitable unloading parties aaa 86th Bde M. Gun Coy to be at Suez Docks at 1100 89th Fd Amb at 1130 Cyclist Coy at 1200 16th Sanitary Section at 1300 aaa Ships adjutant SM OMS and 6 OR to be at Embarkation Office Suez Docks at 0900 with nominal rolls and embarkation list in duplicate of all embarking aaa Units will have their nominal rolls & return in to Capt Beckmk R Fus by 0730 on 16th aaa Units will also arrange to send nominal rolls of all their officers to be at Embarkation Off by 07. so their cabins may be allotted aaa Reference para 6 of yesterdays orders the arrangements for meals is confirmed aaa The Sanitary Section will head in

From
Place
Time

"A" Form.   Army Form
MESSAGES AND SIGNALS.   No. of Message

Men proceed with all Embarkation returns
to the Chiefs Adjutant at the Embarkation
office at Suez Docks at 0900 and similarly
the names of the officer at 0900 to the
Embarkation office aaa addressed 88th Bde
M.G. Coy 89th Field Ambulance OC Cyclists
OC 16th Sanitary Section repeated Embarkation
officer Suez Docks.

From 29th Div
Time 1245

Name of Ship.	Place and Date of Embarkation.	Name of Unit.	Officers.	O Ranks.	Horses.
KAROA.	Alexandria. on March 9th.	132nd How. R.F.A.	13	315	320
		S.W.Borderers.	20	300	
		95th Fld Amb.	1	73	
		Records & Base Depot.	2	40	
		64th D.U.S.	1	13	
		Totals.	37	741	320
KINGSTONIAN &	Alexandria. on March 9th.	17th Bde.R.F.A.	20	481	557
		15th Bde.R.H.A.	9	222	125
		2/S.W.B.	8	224	2
		1/K.O.S.B. (Officers Chargers)		2	2
		1/Border		2	2
		1/R.Inns.Fus.		1	1
		87th Bde H.Qrs.	4	4	4
		29th Div H.Qrs.		1	1
		29th Div.R.A.		4	4
		Div.Engineers.H.Q.		3	3
		Div.Signal Coy.		2	2
		88th Brigade.		6	6
		86th Brigade.		5	5
		R.E.		4	4
		Mobile Vety.Section.		3	3
		Totals.	37	1037	1064
HUANCHACO	Alexandria on March 9th.	15th Bde.R.H.A.	10	200	448

Name of Ship.	Place & Date of Embarkation.	Name of Unit.	Offs.	O.Ranks.
WANDILLA	Suez	1/K.O.S.B.	23	596
	10th March, 1916.	87th M.G.Coy.	1	48
		1/R.Innis.Fus.	31	699
		Chaplains	3	
			58	1343
MEGANTIC.	Port Said	1/K.O.S.B.	10	368
	11th March, 1916.	87th Bde.Hqrs.	3	34
		x	13	402
WARILDA.	Suez.	1/Border Rgt.	31	930
	11th March, 1916.	x 87th M.G.Coy.	8	137
		18th Vety.Sectn.	1	21
		88th F.Amb.	11	200
		2/London Co.R.E.	7	139
		192nd D.U.S.	1	13
		203rd D.U.S.	1	13
		232nd D.U.S.	1	13
		358th D.U.S.	1	13
			62	1479
ELELE.	Alexandria	132~ ~~crxxx~~ How.Bde	12	200 horses 550
	11th March 1916.	147ᵗ F.A Bde	4	300
			16	500 horses 550
MENOMINEE	Alexandria	Div.Sig.Coy,	6	163
	12th March,	Div.Engnrs.Hqrs.	3	9
	1916.	1/Dublin Fus.	27	659
		Arty.Reinforcemts.		100
		147th Bde R.F.A.	16	209 horses 250
		Remainder of horses 29th Divn.		{189 {33 WS horses 60
			52	1175 horses WWO
		x		472

		2nd Flight		
Abassieh	Suez	2nd Royal Fus.	29	906
~~Kaisar-i-Hind~~		1st R. Munster Fus.	24	290
March 18th		Chaplain	1	—
		W. Kent Fd Coy	5	153
		Newfoundland Bn.	25	577
			84	1926

		3rd Flight		
Lake Manitoba	Suez	16th Sanitary Section	1	37
		Machine Gun Coy 86 Bde	9	106
		89th Fd Amb.ce	10	226
		Div. HQ	2	3
		~~1st Royal Scots~~	26	308
		Div. Amm Col. Personnel	1	35
		Cyclist Coy	×2	215
		Records Section	2	32
		Divl Signal Co. (Balance)	×2	30
			6929	987
				684

Transylvania	Alexandria	88th Bde. M.G. Co.	8	138
	15th Mar.	88th Bde HQ	2	33
		4th Worc. Regt.	30	814
		2nd Hants "	27	924
		1st Essex "	28	1009
		Chaplain	1	—
			96 ×	2918

Miltiades	Suez,	Div HQ	8	57
	March 13th	R.A HQ	6	20
		1/W. Riding Fd Coy.	7	160
		87th Fd Amb.	9	247
		1/Lanc Fus.	33	704
		86th Brig. HQ	4	32
		Band		30
			67	1250

appx 14

Appendix 14.

BILLETS - 29th. DIVISION.

Divl Hd Qtrs.	LONG.	In Chateau.
" Band.	"	Out-houses of Chateau
" Cyclist Coy.	"	Cafe Francais
" Signal Coy.	"	In village.
" Sanitary Section.	"	do.

Surrey Yeomanry	BROCAMPS.	
Divl. Artillery Hd.Qtrs.	COCQUEREL.	In Chateau.
15th. Bde. R.H.A.	ETOILE.	
369th. Battery.	BOUCHON.	
Bde Amm. Col.	~~CONDE~~. *ETOILE*	
17th. Bde. R.F.A.)	LONG *& LONGUET*	
370th. Battery)		
132nd. Bde R.F.A.	PONT REMY.	
147th. " "	VAUCHELLES LES DOMART.	
371st. Battery.	MOUFLERS.	
Bde. Amm. Col.	VILLERS SOUS AILLY.	
Divl. Amm. Col.	~~CONDE~~. *PONT REMY & Francieres*	
R.E. Hd. Qtrs.	AILLY LE HAUT CLOCHER.	In Chateau.
London Field Coy.	BUSSUS-BUSSUE.	
Kent Field Coy.	MONTFLIERS near BELLANCOURT.	
West Riding Field Co.	SURCAMPS.	
86th. Infantry Bde)	DOMQUEUR.	
H.Q. M.G. Co.)		
Royal Fusilers.	COULON VILLERS.	
Lancs "	BUSSUS-BUSSUE.	
Munster "	MAISON ROLLAND.	
Dublin "	DOMQUEUR. *Surcamps*	
87th. Bde Hd. Qtrs.)	GORENFLOS.	
M.G. Coy.)		
S.W.B's)	DOMART.	
K.O.S.B's)		
R. Innis. Fus.	ERGNIES.	
Border Regt.	GORENFLOS.	
88th. Infantry Bde H.Q.	BOIS DE L'ABBEY.	
M.G. Coy.	BELLANCOURT.	
Worcester Regt.	YAUCOURT BUSSUS.	
Hants Regt.	VAUCHELLES LES QUESNOY.	
Essex Regt.	BELLANCOURT.	
1/5th. Royal Scots.	AILLIEL.	
Newfoundland Bn.	BUIGNY L'ABBE.	
87th. Field Ambulance.	~~SURCAMPS~~. *Gorenflos*	
88th. " "	BELLANCOURT.	In Chateau.
89th. " " :	MAISON ROLLAND.	
Divl. Train)	AILLY LE HAUT CLOCHER.	
Mobile Vet. Section.)	*Pont REMY*	
Divl Supply Col	*Mouflers.*	

Copy No. 1.   SECRET.

VIII CORPS OPERATION ORDER NO. 2

26th March, 1916.

Reference, Fourth Army Administrative Map attached (extracted & hung on wall)
and Trench Map 1/10,000 Sheets 57 D. N.E. 3 & 4 (parts of)
and 57 D. S.E. 1 & 2 (parts of).

1.   On 30th March, 29th Division will commence moving from present billetting area to Reserve Area, VIII Corps.

        The Division is to be concentrated in VIII Corps Reserve Area by evening of 2nd April.

2. (a)   On 2nd April, 29th Division will commence taking over from 31st Division the front from Q.17.c.7.3 to Q.4.b.Central.

   (b)   On same date 31st Division will commence to take over from 48th Division the front from present right of 48th Division to North end of MARK COPSE, inclusive, K.29.a.10.8.

3.   The Artillery of 29th Division will relieve that portion of the artillery of 31st Division covering the 29th Division front. Similarly, Artillery of 31st Division will relieve that portion of Artillery 48th Division covering 31st Division front. Relief to commence after completion of Infantry Relief. Detailed orders regarding Artillery relief will be issued by G.O.C., R.A., VIII Corps.

4.   Arrangements for relief and reconnaissance of new fronts to be made direct between Divisions concerned. Reliefs, except Artillery relief, to be completed by night of April 5th/6th. by which date Divisions are to be concentrated in the billetting areas shown on map issued herewith.

5.   On completion of relief the fronts held by Divisions will be as follows:-

    (a) 29th Division, Q.17.c.7.3 to Q.4.b.Central,
        Southern Boundary - Present X Corps Boundary.
        Northern Boundary - Q.4.b.Central - Q.3.a.7.7.
        Q.2.b.46. Thence as in billetting map.
        Div. H.Q. ACHEUX.

(b)

(2)

    (b)   31st Division, Q.4.b.Central to K.29.a.10.8
             Northern Boundary - K.29.a.10.8 - K.28.b.48-
             - K.28.a.45. Thence as in billetting map.
             Div. H.Q., BUS LES ARTOIS.

    (c)   48th Division, K.29.a.10.8 to present left.
             Northern Boundary - as at present.
             Div. H.Q. COUIN.

6.   A list is attached giving suggested billetting arrangements for 29th ~~and 31st~~ Divisions in the new areas but G.O.C's are at liberty to alter the arrangements within their areas as they may consider desirable.

7.   Acknowledge.

8.   Please note that Chateau at ACHEUX will not be available for 29th Div. H.Q. till morning April 3rd

                      W. Ruttven   B.G., G.S.
                                  VIII Corps.

Issued to Signals at

        Copy No. 1   29th Division.
                 2   31st Division.
                 3   48th Division.
                 4   A.D.C. to Corps Commander.
              5-6   War Diary.
                 7   File.
                 8   "Q".
                 9   G.O.C., R.A.
               10   C.E.
               11   A.P.M.
               12   D.D.M.S.
               13   VIII Corps Signals.
               14   Fourth Army (for information).
               15   VII Corps (for information).
               16   X Corps (for information).

29th DIVISION.

SUGGESTIONS.

INFANTRY.

- 3 Battns. — Front & AUCHONVILLERS.
- 1 " — ENGLEBELMER.
- 1 " — MAILLY-MAILLET.
- 1 " for Mining — do —
- 1 " — BEAUSSART
- 2 " — ACHEUX
- 1 " — BELLE EGLISE & ARQUEVES
- 3 " — LOUVENCOURT.

ENGINEERS.

- 1 Field Co. ENGLEBELMER
- 1 " " MAILLY MAILLET.
- 1 " " ACHEUX.

ARTILLERY.

Battery Wagon Lines Inwoods about ENGLEBELMER and MAILLY MAILLET: ACHEUX.

- B.A.C's ACHEUX & LOUVENCOURT.
- D.A.C. ORVILLE.

MOUNTED TROOPS. AMPLIER

FIELD AMBULANCES

- 2 .... ACHEUX
- 1 .... ARQUEVES

TRAIN VAUCHELLES

M V S VAUCHELLES

SUPPLY COLUMN FRESCHEVILLERS.

29th Division.

Village.	ACCOMMODATION.				WATER.	Suggested allotment
	In ordinary billets.	In completed huts.	Total ordinary conditions	Extra for close billets		
Front and AUCHONVILLERS.)						3 Battalions
ENGLEBELMER	1300	-	1500	690	5 Wells. Also use MAILLY	1 Battn. 1 Field Co, Battery Wagon Lines in Wood
MAILLY MAILLET	3000	-	3000	1800	Power pump 18000 gls per 8 hour day. 1 Stand pipe for water carts, 2 horse trough systems	1 Battn, 1 Battn. for wiring 1 Fld Co, Battery Wagon Lines in Wood.
BEAUSSART	350	-	350	450	2 Wells, 1600 galls per 8 hour day	1 Battalion.
ACHEUX	2200	1870	3070 (4370)	1300	Power pump, 24000 galls per 8 hour day. 4 stand pipes for water carts. 1 horse trough system. (Railway will require 12000 galls daily)	2 Battns. 1 Field Co. 2 Fld.Amb. Battery Wagon Lines, B.A.C's
BELLE EGLISE Fm	350	-	650	350	1 Well, 800 galls per 8 hour) day.	1 Battalion, 1 Field Amb.
ARQUEVES	500	-	500	700	Wells, Persian wheel & tank)	
LOUVENCOURT	3500	240	3740	600	About 25 wells. 15000 galls per 8 hour day.	3 Battalions. B.A.C's
VAUCHELLES	800	1150	1950	500	13 Wells. Pump for 1500 horses	Train. M.V.S. also Train and M.V.S. of 31st Division.
ORVILLE	1400	-	1400	1800	2000 horses left bank 2000 horses right bank	D.A.C. also D.A.C. 31st Div.
FRESCHEVILLERS				200		Supply Column, also Supply Column of 31st Division.
AMPLIER	500	4440	4940		2000 horses by power pump from river. 130' well with 300 g.p.h.hand pumps.	Mounted troops, also Mounted Troops 31st Divn.

Appx. 15

SECRET.   COPY NO. 3

Appendix 15

OPERATION ORDER NO. 23
by
Major General H.de B.de Lisle, C.B.,D.S.O.
Commanding 29th Division.

28th March 1916.

Reference Fourth
Army Administrative
Map.

1. On the 30th March the 87th Brigade Group and 132nd Brigade R.F.A. will move to new billets as shown in the attached list and March Table 'A'.

2. Re-filling point on the 30th March, AILLY 8.0 am.

3. Orders referring to R.F.A and A.S.C are cancelled.

W. M. Armstrong   Captain, G.S.
                  29th Division.

Issued at _____

Copy No. 1   Divisional H.Q.
        2   "   "
        3   "   "
        4   Headquarters, R.A.
    5 - 8   Artillery Brigades.
        9   86th Brigade
       10   87th   "
       11   88th   "
       12   C.R.E.
       13   8th Corps.

29TH DIVISION.

BILLETS IN 8TH CORPS RESERVE AREA.

Divisional Headquarters	BEAUQUESNE.
R.E. Headquarters	"
Temporary Supply Train	"
Ammunition Sub Park	"
Mobile Veterinary Section	"
Surrey Yeomanry	HEM
Divisional Artillery H.Q.	FRESCHEVILLERS
15th Bde. R.H.A.	"
17th Bde. R.F.A.	ORVILLE
No. 3 Coy. A.S.C.	"
132nd Bde. R.F.A.	SARTON
Divisional Ammunition Column	"
147th Bde. R.F.A.	GERAINCOURT
Nos. 1 & 2 Coys. A.S.C.	"

86th Infantry Brigade.

3 Battalions	BEAUVAL
Kent R.E.	"
89th Field Ambulance	"
1 Battalion	CANDAS

87th Infantry Brigade

3 Battalions	AMPLIER
West Riding R.E.	"
87th Field Ambulance	"
1 Battalion	BEAUQUESNE

88th Infantry Brigade

4 Battalions)(	MONTRELET
88th Field Ambulance)(	FIEFFES
No. 4 Coy. A.S.C.)(	BONNEVILLE
1 Battalion	FIENVILLERS
London R.E.	LONGUE VILLETTE.
Divisional Supply Column	CANDAS.

MARCH TABLE FOR MARCH 30th 1916.

TABLE "A"

Unit.	From.	To.	Route.	Time.	Remarks.
87th Brigade. West Riding R.E. 87th Field Ambulance.	DOMART.	AMPLIER BEAUQUESNE	BERNEUIL - MONTRELET BONNEVILLE - BEAUVAL.	8-0 a.m.	A temporary Group under orders G.O.C. 87th Brigade.

(sgd.) W.M.Armstrong..

Captain G.S.,

29th Division.

april 16

Appendix 16.

SECRET.   Copy No...... 2.

OPERATION ORDER NO 24
by
Major General H. de B. de Lisle C.B.D.S.O.
Commanding 29th Division.

Ref. 4th Army Administrative Map.   30th March 1916.

1. The following units will move on March 31st to new
Billets in accordance with the attached March Table "B":-

    Divisional Headquarters.

    Surrey Yeomanry.

    86th Brigade Group.

R.A. Headquarters →   Mobile Veterinary Section.
    17th Brigade R.F.A.
    15th Brigade R.H.A.
    147th Brigade R.F.A.
    132nd (How.) Brigade R.F.A.
    No. 2 Coy. A.S.C.
    R.E. Headquarters.

2. For March 31st :

    Re-filling point AILLY 8. a.m.

    Re-filling point for 87th Brigade Group

LE BON AIR (1½ miles South of DOUILLES) 10. a.m.

    Railhead CANDAS.

C.J. Fuller, Lieut. Col.
Captain G.S.,
29th Division.

Issued at ......0945......
Copy No. 1-3 Divisional Headquarters.
    4-8 Headquarters R.A.
    9   86th Brigade.
   10   87th Brigade.
   11   88th Brigade.
   12   C.R.E.
   13   8th Corps.

MARCH TABLE "B".

Unit	From	To	Route	Time	Remarks.
Divisional H.Q.	LONG	BEAUQUESNE	L'ETOILE- CANAPLES	8.30 a.m.	
Surrey Yeomanry.	BRUCAMPS	HEM	DOMART-BERNEUIL -CANAPLES	8 a.m.	To be clear of BERNEUIL by 10 a.m.
88th Inf. Brigade	DOEQUEUR	BEAUVAL- CANDAS	FRANQUEVILLE - BERNEUIL - MONTRELET	8 a.m.	To form a temporary group under command of G.O.C. Brigade.
Kent R.E.	SURCAMPS	"	"		
89th Field Ambulance.	MAISON ROLLAND	BEAUVAL	"		
Mobile Vet. Section.	LONG	BEAUQUESNE	LONG-L'ETOILE -CANAPLES	8.30 a.m.	
R.A.Headquarters.	COCQUEREL	DOMART	Shortest Route	9 a.m.	R.F.Brigades to march at ½ hours intervals.
17th Bde.R.F.A.	LONG				
15th Bde. R.H.A.	L'ETOILE				
147th Bde.R.F.A.	VAUCHELLES				
132nd Bde. R.F.A. (How.)	PONT REMY				
No. 2 Coy. A.S.C.	AILLY	BEAUVAL	ARGUCAPS - DOMART	8 a.m.	
R.E.Headquarters.	AILLY	BEAUQUESNE	DOMART-BERNEUIL - BEAUVAL	7.30 a.m.	

C.R. [signature]
Lieut. Colonel, G.S
29th Division.

www.ingramcontent.com/pod-product-compliance
Lightning Source LLC
Chambersburg PA
CBHW080903230426

43664CB00016B/2715